What Does Justice Look Like?

Minisota Makoce. *Photo by Waziyatawin.*

What Does Justice Look Like?

The Struggle for Liberation in Dakota Homeland

Waziyatawin, Ph.D.

Living Justice Press

ST. PAUL, MINNESOTA

Living Justice Press
St. Paul, Minnesota 55105

For information about permission to reproduce selections from this book, please contact:

Permissions, Living Justice Press, 2093 Juliet Avenue, St. Paul, MN 55105
Tel. (651) 695-1008 or contact permissions through our
Web site: www.livingjusticepress.org

Library of Congress Cataloging-in-Publication Data

Wilson, Angela Cavender.
    What does justice look like? : the struggle for liberation in Dakota
homeland / by Waziyatawin. — 1st ed.
        p.   cm.
    ISBN 0-9721886-5-7 (978-0-9721886-5-4)
    1. Indians of North America—Minnesota—Government relations.
2. Indians of North America—Minnesota—Social conditions. 3. Indians,
Treatment of—Minnesota—History. 4. Self-determination, National—
Minnesota. 5. Social justice—Minnesota. 6. Minnesota—Race relations.
7. Minnesota—Social policy. 8. Minnesota—Politics and government.
I. Title.
    E78.M7W553   2008
    323.11970776—dc22
                                                        2008021700

12 11 10 09 08   5 4 3 2 1

Copyediting by Cathy Broberg
Cover design by David Spohn
Interior design by Wendy Holdman
Printed by Sheridan Books, Ann Arbor, Michigan
on Nature's Book recycled paper

Contents

Minisota Makoce. *Photo by Waziyatawin.*

A Note to Readers

I engaged this project to initiate dialogue around outstanding injustices experienced by Dakota people, injustices that the dominant society has yet to either acknowledge or address. While my perspective is always shaped from my identity as a Wahpetunwan Dakota from the Pezihutazizi K'api Makoce (Land Where They Dig for Yellow Medicine), my perspective is not reflective of all people from my community, my council fire, or my nation. Thus, I do not claim to be speaking for all Wahpetunwan people, all people from Yellow Medicine, or all Dakota people. I am just one person, offering suggestions for an alternative vision of the future that would allow Dakota people to reclaim our homeland and live once again as a free and independent people.

The ideas contained here developed from multiple life experiences. First, they stem from my critical reading of the history of our Minnesota homeland based on my experience as someone who grew up in the Dakota oral tradition and someone who studied the academic discipline of history. Second, they stem from my awareness of the oppression that Dakota people continue to experience every single day. Severe oppression did not end in the nineteenth century, as many believe. Rather, settler society continues the oppression of Dakota people through the perpetuation of colonialism and the ongoing denial of our inherent rights as Indigenous People of this land. Third, these ideas stem from my beliefs about what is right, what is just, and what is good. Finally and most importantly, the ideas included here are an expression of my hope for the future.

I thank all the people who supported the creation of this volume through their contributions to Living Justice Press. They include the Upper Sioux and Lower Sioux Dakota Communities, the Minnesota Humanities Center, the HRK Foundation, the Patrick and Aimee Butler Family Foundation, and the Archie D. and Bertha H. Walker Foundation. The individuals involved with these communities and institutions do not necessarily support all the views contained in this book, but they do support the need to give voice to the often-ignored perspectives of Indigenous Peoples.

I also want to thank Denise Breton and everyone at Living Justice Press for believing in this project. It is so essential for Dakota people to have an outlet to express our critical perspectives in our own voices and in our own ways. Nina wopida eciciyapi!

In writing this book, I must emphasize that I do not intend it to be a blueprint that everyone must follow. Rather, it is my hope that it will serve as a jumping-off point for discussions in both Dakota and White communities about how we might all achieve a state of peaceful co-existence with each other and with the land we inhabit. No one will agree with everything written here. However, I hope all of you will find at least some truth you can embrace that will lead you to join us in the Dakota struggle for justice.

Waziyatawin
Pezihutazizi Otunwe
February 15, 2008

〰 What Does Justice Look Like?

St. Croix River, Minnesota. *Photo by Waziyatawin.*

Envisioning Justice in Minnesota

Until America begins to build a moral record in her dealings with the Indian people she should try not to fool the rest of the world about her intentions on other continents. America has always been a militantly imperialistic world power eagerly grasping for economic control over weaker nations. . . . There has not been a time since the founding of the republic when the motives of this country were innocent.[1]

— VINE DELORIA JR.

In 2008, the State of Minnesota is celebrating 150 years of statehood. Parades, festivities, and much whoopla are accompanying this important anniversary in Minnesota history. The state government, institutions, and appointed Sesquicentennial Commission are asking all of us to reflect on what Minnesotans have *gained* in the last century and a half as well as what *progress* Minnesotans have achieved. Minnesota's original inhabitants, the Dakota Oyate (Nation), have a different perspective on those 150 years. Rather than measuring the years by what we have gained, Dakota people more often measure what we have *lost.* We ask ourselves such questions as

• What does it mean that settler society established the State of Minnesota at the expense of Indigenous Peoples?

- What does it mean that Minnesota's citizens advocated, supported, and perpetrated genocidal policies
  so they could obtain Dakota homeland?
- What does it mean that Dakota extermination and
  forced removal (as well as Ho-Chunk removal) were
  the price of Minnesota's statehood?
- And, what does it mean in the twenty-first century
  when Minnesotans celebrate the establishment of the
  state, despite its shameful historical legacy and the
  harmful consequences to whole nations of Indigenous
  Peoples?

Addressing Harms Internationally

We pose these questions at a time when the international community is beginning to address both the historical harms perpetrated against Indigenous Peoples globally and the contemporary
harms we suffer because of ongoing subjugation and oppression.
On September 13, 2007, the General Assembly of the United
Nations adopted the Declaration on the Rights of Indigenous
Peoples with an overwhelming majority. This declaration affirms
both the individual and collective rights of Indigenous people
as a way to promote justice and peace for all human beings
throughout the world without discrimination. Article 8 of the
declaration is particularly relevant to the discussion of Minnesota history:

1. Indigenous peoples and individuals have the right not
   to be subjected to forced assimilation or destruction
   of their culture.
2. States shall provide effective mechanisms for prevention of, and redress for:
   (a) Any action which has the aim or effect of depriv-
   ing them of their integrity as distinct peoples, or
   of their cultural values or ethnic identities;

(b) Any action which has the aim or effect of dispossessing them of their lands, territories or resources;

(c) Any form of forced population transfer which has
the aim or effect of violating or undermining any
of their rights;

(d) Any form of forced assimilation or integration;

(e) Any form of propaganda designed to promote
or incite racial or ethnic discrimination directed
against them.

Every one of these applies to the internationally recognized crimes
perpetrated by Minnesota citizens and the United States government against the Dakota people of Minnesota to obtain Dakota
lands and resources as well as eliminate our populations. By eliminating or severely debilitating the original owners of the land and
its resources, White Minnesotans ensured that Dakota people
could no longer threaten the genocidal and exploitative policies
that would continue to enrich them and other U.S. citizens.

Article 8 of the declaration directly challenges Minnesota's
right to establish itself at the expense of Indigenous Peoples. It
dictates that the United States (as the State) and Minnesota have
an obligation to acknowledge and ensure some kind of reparative justice for these harms. Furthermore, the declaration would
certainly condemn the celebration of that which was gained at
the expense of Indigenous populations such as the Dakota. In
this context, Minnesota's decision to celebrate the sesquicentennial is completely out of sync with an international community
committed to working toward peace and justice.

In fact, rather than celebrating, other world powers are apol-
ogizing for their treatment of Indigenous Peoples. On February
13, 2008, as the first item of business for Australia's new parliament, Prime Minister Kevin Rudd apologized to Aboriginal
Australians for the "laws and policies of successive parliaments
and governments that have inflicted profound grief, suffering and loss on these our fellow Australians."[2] He apologized

especially to the stolen generations of Aboriginal children forcibly removed from their families because of federal policies that lasted through the late 1960s.

Like Indigenous Peoples in the United States, Australian Aborigines comprise only a small percentage of the population (2 percent), yet they suffer the highest rates of infant mortality, drug abuse, alcoholism, and unemployment. Many hope the apology will "allow Australia to re-commit to improving the lives of Indigenous people."[3] In the best-case scenario, this apology would mark just the beginning of a long process toward creating Aboriginal justice in Australia. It remains to be seen, however, whether the country will act on the apology, or if they will remain just words. As the Aboriginal leader Noel Pearson put it, "Blackfellas will get the words, the Whitefellas keep the money."[4] Still this event is now part of a worldwide discourse regarding truth telling, acknowledgement of harms, and reparative justice.

Frankly, it is more comfortable for White Minnesotans to consider what is happening to Indigenous Peoples in other parts of the world, rather than to investigate what is happening to Indigenous Peoples in their own backyard. Minnesota's restorative justice workers, for example, frequently empathize with suffering elsewhere and join in the global chorus of voices demanding justice for oppressed Peoples across the oceans. They help victims and offenders engage in transformative healing practices elsewhere while condemning violence and holding perpetrators of harms accountable for their actions. Meanwhile, the monumental harms perpetrated against Dakota people remain unacknowledged and unaddressed. Yet, all Minnesotans continue to benefit from Dakota dispossession and every day they continue to deny justice to Dakota people.

The Minnesota Context

In this volume, I will center the focus on the land we call home. I will offer Minnesotans an alternative, ethically grounded way to think about the historical legacy created by the establishment of Minnesota statehood and the ongoing oppression experienced by Dakota people. Within a contemporary context, I will also address the difficult questions posed at the beginning of this chapter. Most importantly, I will address how the beneficiaries of genocide in this instance might begin to undo the damages wrought from gross injustices. This includes a plan to return Dakota people to our homeland as well as restore the integrity of the landscape so that we can create some semblance of justice in Minnesota.

Ho-Chunk people have a similar legitimate claim to justice in Minnesota as co-victims of Minnesota's ethnic cleansing policy. However, only Ho-Chunk people can speak to the objectives of their struggle and articulate their vision for a liberated future. Thus, for this project, I will specifically address Dakota concerns from a Dakota perspective.

In addition, given Minnesota's largely unfettered celebration of statehood in 2008, it is clear there is a desperate need for reflection on the meaning of Minnesota statehood in the context of a genocidal and oppressive historical legacy. This book will thus utilize the rhetoric surrounding Minnesota's sesquicentennial to illuminate White ignorance regarding the contemporary Dakota struggle for justice. Perhaps then Minnesotans will understand why their ongoing celebration of what was gained at Dakota expense is just another assault on Dakota humanity.

Another provocative backdrop for this project is the current lawsuit filed against the federal government on behalf of 7,500 descendants of the "loyal Mdewakanton." In May 2004, a group of Dakota people held a constitutional convention in Redwood Falls, Minnesota, to create and approve a new constitution as well as to elect officers to establish the Minnesota Mdewakanton Dakota Oyate. These individuals are descendants of a small segment of Bdewakantunwan Dakota who were loyal to the United States government during the U.S.–Dakota War of 1862.[5] The government allowed this small group to remain in Minnesota and eventually provided land to them as a reward for their loyalty, but only on the condition that they would sever all tribal ties.

Today, the descendants of those "loyal Mdewakanton," claim that the other Bdewakantunwan living on lands in Minnesota are wrongful beneficiaries of three Dakota reservations reserved specifically for them. They have filed a suit in the United States Court of Federal Claims (Sheldon Peters Wolfchild, Ernie Peters Longwalker, Scott Adolphson, Morris J. Pendleton, Barbara Feezor Buttes, et al. vs. United States, Case No. 03-2684-L) to "recover damages for Defendant's trust mismanagement, breach of trustee fiduciary duties and breach of contract by the defendant." Ultimately, they want those parcels of land back (and everything on the land), exclusively for the descendants of the "Loyal Mdewakanton."

While the success of their lawsuit has yet to be determined, the considerable support for the lawsuit among Dakota people suggests that there is a popular desire for land restoration in Minnesota. It clearly indicates that land issues are by no means settled in Dakota eyes. Yet, there are also implications of this lawsuit that may be detrimental to the Dakota struggle for justice. I will address the negative implications of the lawsuit in the last portion of this book.

In light of these two major events—Minnesota's sesquicentennial and the "Loyal Mdewakanton" lawsuit—it is clear that we need a vision for an alternative future in this place we call *Minisota*. At this reflective moment, it is useful for everyone— the populations of people who colonized Dakota lands as well as Dakota people in Minnesota and in exile—to consider their roles, ideas, expectations, and hopes for the future in the context of a broad view of Minnesota history. This book attempts to provide one such revisioning with the hope that it will generate useful discussions, deep reflection, and subsequent action. Neither Dakota people nor the non-Dakota people who call our homeland theirs have ever engaged in a collective discussion or debate about the meaning of Minnesota statehood. Furthermore, we have not engaged in public discussions with an eye toward truthfully exploring what White Minnesotans gained at the expense of Indigenous Peoples. With this work, I hope to foster that collective discussion among all Minnesota populations.

In chapter 1, I will provide an historical overview of *Minisota Makoce* from the Dakota perspective. Dakota people consider Minnesota the site of our creation and we have existed on this particular land base for thousands of years. It is Dakota homeland. No other population in the world can claim this deep connection to Minnesota. Because I cannot explore this long history in depth in a single text, this chapter will only briefly highlight the nature of this ancient relationship. It will also explain how White Minnesotans violently and painfully wrested the land out of Dakota hands as well as the subsequent painful repercussions to both Dakota people and the land. Rather than providing detailed chronological accounts of the history of Dakota-White relations, I will place special emphasis on categories of human injustices perpetrated against Dakota people that I will illuminate with specific examples. I will conclude this chapter with a discussion of the conditions resulting from this painful legacy within Dakota communities and a discussion about what this tells us about our relationship to settler society.

Following the discussion of the historical and contemporary context for examining a restoration of justice in Dakota homeland, this book will then address four possible stages for reparative justice: the establishment of a Truth Commission in the state of Minnesota; the need for a process to "Take Down the Fort"; a program of land restoration and reparations; and, finally, the end of American colonization of Dakota people and homeland. While these dramatic stages may seem radical and impossible, they are, in fact, essential to creating a moral and just society in which Dakota and non-Dakota can peacefully co-exist and respectfully share this place we call *Minisota Makoce*.

Despite the fact that Minnesota's ethnic cleansing of Dakota and Ho-Chunk Peoples is well documented, most Minnesotans remain naively or purposefully ignorant of the reality that violent and morally reprehensible crimes were perpetrated so they could not only freely obtain Indigenous lands, but could also settle on them without fear of any violent retribution. The genocidal practices such as the mass hanging of Dakota resisters, the forced removal of both Dakota and Ho-Chunk Nations, the bounties placed on Dakota scalps, and the punitive expeditions sent to hunt down the fleeing Dakota, all have left disturbing and devastating legacies.

This is precisely why we cannot put this history behind us. The contemporary circumstances compel us to look at the root causes of our current dysfunction and pain. Many people, even Dakota people, believe it is time for us to put all this terrible history behind us and move on, but our contemporary problems suggest deep-rooted pain. Furthermore, when we expose the root causes of our pain and question whether those root causes still affect our lives, we see that the same oppression facing our people in the nineteenth century still exists today.

For example, the vast majority of Dakota people still live in exile. That is, most of our people still have no home in our ancestral homeland. In addition, nascent Dakota communities (inside and outside the state boundaries) are plagued with horrendous social conditions, such as high substance use and abuse rates, high rates of family violence including physical and sexual abuse, high mortality and suicide rates, high rates of high school dropouts, and high rates of disease. This, of course, is not attributable solely to Minnesota's extermination policies, but those policies laid the groundwork for subsequent and extraordinarily successful colonization of the people. Today's social conditions are a direct result of those combined processes. Thus, to put the past behind us requires turning a blind eye to both the ongoing injustices and the ongoing effects of colonization.

Furthermore, the ethnic cleansing of Dakota and Ho-Chunk Peoples out of Minnesota was extraordinarily successful. In fact, the ethnic cleansing of the Ho-Chunk nation was so successful that they have no formally designated land base in the state of Minnesota today. Similarly, the land base for Dakota people today can only be considered outrageously small, given the breadth of the boundaries of our ancestral homeland. Today we hold approximately 3,200 acres out of what used to be millions of acres, making our four Dakota communities tiny dots on the map. Yet, settler society has not held itself accountable for their part in the ongoing denial of justice. In fact, settler society has routinely silenced, suppressed, or denied Dakota and Ho-Chunk accounts detailing our experiences as victims of crimes against humanity.

Initiating an Era of Truth Telling

A truth-telling forum, therefore, would allow us to bring those accounts to the forefront of the consciousness of the settler society in the state of Minnesota. This would disallow Minnesotans from denying or ignoring the history of genocide and the perpetration of human injustices. The sesquicentennial offers an ideal time to initiate a new era of truth telling in Minnesota to counter the 150 years of myth making.

Taking Down the Fort

Awareness of truth, however, compels some kind of action. Once settler society acknowledges injustices and demonstrates some sort of contrition, they will create a moral imperative for restorative justice. The process of restorative justice is perhaps more easily conceived in stages. Once we initiate a phase of truth telling, it will necessarily cause us to rethink the foundations upon which the state of Minnesota was created. One of those foundations is that the "settlement" of Indigenous land is benign or even benevolent. When the violence and nastiness of the imperial business is unmasked, we must question the morality of continuing to celebrate Minnesota's imperial and colonial icons. With that unmasking, not only do we realize that we cannot celebrate those icons, we also realize we must pursue a campaign to "Take Down the Fort," both literally and metaphorically. While this phrase applies most tangibly to historic Fort Snelling, the site of the Dakota concentration camp during the winter of 1862–63, it also applies to all monuments, institutions, place names, and texts that continue to celebrate the perpetrators of genocide or the institutions and systems that facilitated the implementation of genocidal and unjust policies.

Making Reparations

To create a moral society, Minnesotans and Americans must then engage the next step in the movement toward reparative justice: land restoration and reparations. While this usually invokes tremendous fear within settler society, there are ways to conceive of land return that do not involve current settlers to relinquish their individual property rights, unless they wish to do so in the name of justice. We can identify more than 11 million acres within the state of Minnesota currently designated as federal, state, county, or metro-commissioned lands. Settler society could immediately return those millions of acres to Dakota People without touching a single acre of privately held lands.

Land return alone, however, is not enough to create justice. Instead, Minnesotans also have to restore those lands to a pristine condition. This would require extensive cleanup efforts, particularly on the part of corporations, farmers, and resource extractors who have left horrendous environmental destruction in the wake of their activities. Together, we will need to address systematically all of these issues. The reality is, however, that restitution for land theft—no matter how long ago the crime was perpetrated—eventually requires land return.

In addition, non-land-based reparations will also be a necessary element of restoring justice in Dakota homeland. Once settler society guarantees a land base to Dakota People, for example, we can then negotiate a system to cover relocation expenses for populations in exile. I would argue that monetary compensation should not be the end goal, but what we need instead is essential support for the creation and development of an Indigenous infrastructure that will allow Dakota People to live according to our values and worldviews.

Creating an Oppression-Free Society

In the end, however, none of this makes sense if institutions and systems of colonization remain in place. Ultimately, if Minnesotans, and Americans in general, are going to create a peaceful and just society, all oppression must cease. Colonization, by its very nature, is antithetical to justice. Therefore, complete decolonization is a necessary end goal in a peaceful and just society. This would entail overturning the institutions, systems, and ideologies of colonialism that continue to affect every aspect of Indigenous life. In a nutshell, we all must rethink our ways of being and interacting in this world to create a sustainable, healthy, and peaceful co-existence with one another and with the natural world.

Human beings are on the cusp of a great change in the world. The flourishing of empire has advanced societal models based on principles of domination, exploitation, and violence. This has served to harm human beings, plants, and animals, as well as the air, lands and waters, thereby pushing us into a planetary crisis. Today we are witnessing the beginning of catastrophic collapses of the existing systems, both natural and man-made, as empire is ultimately self-destructive. But, we have a choice. As author David Korten relates, this transformation "can play out in the mode of Empire, as a violent, self-destructive, last-man-standing competition for individual advantage. Or it can play out in the mode of Earth Community, as a cooperative effort to rebuild community; to learn the arts of sufficiency, sharing, and peaceful conflict resolution; and to marshal our human creativity to grow the generative potential of the whole."[6] I, for one, would prefer the latter option. If Minnesotans choose Earth Community, it will require all of us to rework the existing social order and to adopt a new set of values based on mutual respect and sustainability.

Contemplating this future requires expansive thinking on the part of all of us. For non-Dakota people, it asks that you challenge, re-examine, and reject the racist and colonialist programming to which you have grown accustomed. It also asks that you rethink the values of domination, consumption, and exploitation that have become a part of American society. For Dakota people, it requires that we awaken our consciousness to the potential for liberation. Most importantly, however, it requires all of us to move beyond a simple re-education and acknowledgment of past harms. It requires action that will fundamentally alter the current power imbalance. It requires action that will serve to ensure justice to the Original People of this place we call *Minisota*.

Note

1. Vine Deloria Jr., *Custer Died for Your Sins: An Indian Manifesto* (Norman: University of Oklahoma Press, 1988), 51. Originally published: New York: Macmillan, 1969.

2. "Australia apology to Aborigines," BBC News, February 13, 2008, http://news.bbc.co.uk/2/hi/asia-pacific/7241965.stm (accessed February 13, 2008).

3. "Government promises action after apology," Australia Broadcasting Corporation (ABC) News, Wednesday, February 13, 2008, http://www.abc.net.au/news/stories/2008/02/13/2161776.htm (accessed February 13, 2008).

4. "Australia apology to Aborigines," BBC News, February 13, 2008, http://news.bbc.co.uk/2/hi/asia-pacific/7241965.stm (accessed February 13, 2008).

5. The legal term for the council fire we call the "Dwellers by Mystic Lake" is Mdewakanton. The Shakopee Mdewakanton Sioux Com-

munity also uses this version. In this volume, outside of quotations or specific names for communities, I will use the term Bdewakantunwan. This version is based on the orthography created by the Dakota-English Dictionary Project in the 1980s and it uses the letter "B" to reflect the "B" sound, replacing the "M" frequently used by the early missionaries to reflect a "B" sound. The different ending is indicative of traditional Dakota speech, rather than an anglicized, contracted version.

6. David Korten, *The Great Turning: From Empire to Earth Community* (San Francisco: Berrett-Koehler Publishers, Inc., 2006), 63.

ONE

How Minnesotans Wrested the Land from Dakota People

The Sioux Indians must be exterminated or driven forever beyond the borders of the State.

— GOVERNOR ALEXANDER RAMSEY, 1862

Banishment from the homeland, the diaspora of a nation, the exile of a people, and ongoing colonization—these are the legacies Minnesotans and Americans have left to Dakota people. What do these legacies mean to the hearts and spirits of Dakota people? Most of us do not care to think too deeply about them, because the difficulties of everyday living as colonized peoples would be infinitely more difficult if we dwelt in a place of inconsolable grief. So, we do not contemplate at length that place of pain and grief and we attempt to avert our eyes when it is brought to our attention. Indeed, even non-colonized people prefer not to dwell in this history because it has the potential to fill them with grief, outrage, guilt, and despair.

Today, I am going to ask you, the reader, to join me on a journey into that dreaded place. I want you to contemplate it with me, experience the sense of moral indignation, and, finally, emerge with a strengthened spirit ready to engage in the Dakota struggle for justice. In the end, it is my hope that we might restore the humanity of everyone.

A Story of Dakota Creation

First, however, I want to share with you a story. This is the creation story of the *Bdewakantunwan* (Dwellers by Mystic Lake)

recounted from memory as I heard respected storyteller Dale
Childs tell it on many occasions. Mr. Childs was from the Prairie Island Reservation located in southeastern Minnesota, and
though he passed away a number of years ago, his stories remain
with us.[1]

A very long time ago, *Wakantanka* (The Great Mystery) created
many children. As he did so, he placed a part of himself into each
being. For instance, he gave the quality of swiftness to the deer,
perseverance to the turtle, strength to the buffalo, and majesty to
the eagle. Every bird, plant, animal, and tree was created so that
each was unique and had a part of *Wakantanka*.

One day, *Wakantanka* was walking in the *Paha Sapa*, or the
Black Hills, and he was looking sad. As he was walking he began
to shed tears. They would fall from his eye and would splash and
dry into nuggets of gold. *Maka*, the Earth, also known as *Ina*,
meaning Mother in our language, wondered why her husband
was sad. She asked, "Have I offended you in some way? Have I
been unfaithful to you? Have I not given you many children?"
When he responded negatively to all those questions, she asked,
"Why then are you looking so sad? Why do I see tears fall?"

Wakantanka replied, "I have many children and they are all
beautiful, but I have another piece of myself to give. When our
children are frightened, they nestle in you for safety. When they
are thirsty, they turn to your waters. And, when they need sus-
tenance, they receive food from your meadows. I want children
who speak to me and call me by name." *Wakantanka* wanted a
creature to look to him for help and to need him.

When *Ina Maka* heard this, she wanted to give a piece of herself to help create a being who would look like her husband. She
called on the waters to help her. She instructed them to come at
her in great magnitude and carve into her flesh. But, the waters
did not want to harm her. She reassured them that they would
not harm her, that it was a gift she wished to give. So they came
at her and began to carve into *Ina*'s body, but the first attempt

was unsuccessful. It didn't work. So she then called on the help of the winds from the four directions. They also refused at first, saying they did not want to harm her. She told them, "You will not harm me. Blow into my body." So the winds agreed. They blew a giant gash into her and exposed the red clay of her body. She called to *Wakantanka*, "My body is open to you. Reach into my body and make a body in the image of yourself."

This was the creation of the first human being. *Ina* told *Wakantanka*, "You will recognize your children. They will be as red as the day. They will call to you, give thanks to you, and share with you your voice." *Wakantanka* put everything into his two-legged children. He gave them love, and the ability to communicate that love. They have a special voice that *Wakantanka* wanted to hear. With that voice we can say, "Thank you for all the blessings," or "On this day I give you thanks." When we are scared, we go to our father and we say, "Look down upon me. Have pity on me. Have pity on my relatives. Help us."

This particular story marks what I believe to be the beginning of interaction between human beings, the river the Dakota refer to as *Hahawakpa* (The River of Falls), and *Minisota Makoce*. In the story I just told, *Ina Maka*, or Mother Earth, instructed the waters to come at her. That first time they were unable to complete their task without the help of the winds. But, in this first attempt, the waters were coming with such force that they created images in rock that could be found along the Mississippi River. Dakota people call the first of those *Caske Tanka* and he is located just south of Red Wing. He was given this name because *Caske* is the name we give to the first-born child in the Dakota family if the child is male, and because *Tanka* means large and this refers to the larger child. Non-Dakota people call this outcropping Barn's Bluff. Dakota people could observe the profile of a Dakota face there until 1954 when settler society dynamited that portion so that they could construct a bridge across the Mississippi River from Minnesota to Wisconsin. Observers can still find another rock image, a little further down river from *Caske Tanka* and it is known as *Caske Cistinna, cistinna* meaning little or small in the Dakota language.

Bdewakantunwan Dakota elders tell of the actual creation of humans occurring in our homeland of *Minisota Makoce*, but specifically at the place called *Maka Cokaya Kin*, or the Center of the Earth. This place is at *Bdote*, which means the joining or juncture of two bodies of water and in this instance refers to the area where the Minnesota River joins the Mississippi. Minnesotans have retained this word as *Mendota* and it is located in the midst of the Twin Cities, with Fort Snelling overlooking the sacred juncture of *Bdote*.

The Dakota people comprise four fires of the *Oceti Sakowin* (Seven Council Fires) that make up the Oyate. They include the *Bdewakantunwan* (Dwellers by Mystic Lake), the *Wahpekute* (Shooters of the Leaves), *Wahpetunwan* (Dwellers Among the Leaves), and the *Sisitunwan* (Dwellers by the Fish Campground).

The creation account I just shared is for Dakota people. I am not sharing it with the expectation that non-Dakota people will subscribe to it or that they will begin to conceive of *Bdote* as their place of origin. Our origin story does not dictate that because the *Bdewakantunwan* emerged at *Bdote*, that all human populations must have emerged there. That is not our way. Instead, the reason I am sharing this story is to demonstrate the ancient and sacred relations we have with this landscape. This is the same sacred and ancient relationship that Christians, Jews, and Muslims have with Middle Eastern sites such as Jerusalem, Mecca, or Nazareth. I am also sharing this story to demonstrate that we do not believe we emigrated from any other place. Rather, our stories assert that we were created here and that we have always lived here. We recognize that we traveled to and lived in other parts of North America over the centuries. We also recognize that our territorial boundaries have fluctuated during the thousands of years we have inhabited this land.[2] And, we recognize that other Indigenous nations shared *Minisota Makoce* with us for periods of time.[3] However, our historical record indicates that there is absolutely no ambiguity about *Minisota* as Dakota homeland.

White Accounts Regarding the Dakota Past

Anthropologists, on the other hand, have proposed a variety of scenarios regarding Dakota presence in Minnesota. They have created an elaborate system of classifications, names, and methods for analyzing Indigenous life before Europeans. University of Minnesota anthropologist Guy Gibbon, for example, has developed a model of "Sioux Prehistory." He based his model on archeological evidence, including the despicable study of Indigenous human remains (obtained without Indigenous consent), and linguistic data. While he admits, "At present, the data upon which this reconstruction of the prehistory of the Sioux is based are weak," he nonetheless asserts the claim that the ancestral "Sioux" arrived from the Central Mississippi Valley shortly before AD 800. Further, he states that it was not until about AD 1300 that we became the People of the Seven Council Fires.

Gibbon's assertions are extremely problematic because they run contrary to every shred of Indigenous evidence and some of his assertions are simply fabrications. This occurs any time academics attempt to imagine the past of another group of human beings based on faulty assumptions (in this case that Dakota people must have originated from elsewhere). Gibbon's assertions run contrary to thousands of years of oral tradition that places Dakota people within *Minisota Makoce*. Furthermore, it is problematic, to say the least, to attribute a cultural (or national) identity to people occupying a specific site based on archeological evidence. Even when ancient cultures leave a different archeological record than more recently dated sites, it does not preclude an ancestral connection between the two. Rather, it may simply indicate that the culture has not been static.

Other archeologists, however, do acknowledge the ancient relationship we have with the land. For example, another twentieth-century scholar, Eldon Johnson, states "The ancestors of the native American groups encountered by the French visitors in the seventeenth century are Minnesota's prehistoric peoples," and this would certainly include the Dakota people.[4]

Still other ethnologists, especially early ones, claim that all the tribes of the Siouan linguistic stock traveled from the East. Royal Hassrick, for example, claims Dakota people arrived from the Northeast, while Albert Jenks asserts that we arrived from the eastern Piedmont and coastal regions of what are now Virginia, North Carolina, and South Carolina before traveling westward to this region (apparently after first arriving via the Bering Strait land bridge and traversing the continent to be positioned on the eastern seashores).[5] Dakota people, however, do not attribute our origins to the eastern seaboard. We also do not attribute our origins to a crossing from Asia via the Bering Strait.

Unfortunately, part of the American imperial enterprise has been to define and rename Indigenous Peoples to diminish our humanity and exploit our resources. In fact, this has been such a dehumanizing practice perpetrated by colonizing powers against Indigenous Peoples that the United Nations Declaration on the Rights of Indigenous Peoples states "Indigenous Peoples have the right to revitalize, use, develop and transmit to future generations their histories, languages, oral traditions, philosophies, writing systems and literatures, and to designate and retain their own names of communities, places and persons."[6] The Dakota Oyate has also been a victim of this radical renaming of people and our landscape.

Anthropologists such as Gibbon, for example, have worked very hard to wrest interpretive control away from Dakota people regarding our own history and origins. They can then supplant our interpretations with their own colonialist vision. This is the ultimate imperial enterprise. Consequently, we have a whole slew of unrecognizable names attributed to Dakota people that include Gibbon's unruly verbiage of bands known as the "Terminal Woodland Blackduck-Kathio-Clam River Continuum."[7] Gibbon is merely carrying on an academic tradition that involves naming the people according to site locations—primarily site locations that colonizing society has already stripped of Indigenous names and supplanted with colonialist names. This only serves to eradicate further Indigenous presence and Indigenous claims. University of Minnesota scholars such as Albert E. Jenks and Lloyd A. Wilford began this practice in Minnesota.[8]

We simply call these populations of people our ancestors. Most people would agree with the notion that Dakota people have the exclusive right to determine who is Dakota today (a right of self-determination that is even held up in U.S. colonial courts), yet most archeologists still unabashedly believe they have a right to define Dakota people of the past regardless of Dakota assertions.

While Dakota oral traditions reach back thousands of years, the first written *Wasicu* (White) records documenting our populations and locations date back to the early French explorers and missionaries of the mid–seventeenth century.[9] Historian Gary Anderson estimates that the population of Dakota people in the Mississippi watershed in 1650 was approximately 38,000, but that by 1780 the population was reduced to about 25,000 due to economic pressures, warfare, and disease. If his estimates are accurate, this indicates a population loss of 35 percent without factoring in normal rates of population growth, all which occurred before massive waves of White invasion.[10]

Anishinabe Invasion

Life began to change radically for Dakota people once French fur traders penetrated Dakota territory and Anishinabe people successfully invaded our northern lands. The Anishinabe were facing European invasion and colonization of their lands in the east, as well as the consequent intertribal warfare characteristic of populations struggling for survival in a rapidly changing landscape. Reasons for Anishinabe migration into Dakota lands are diverse, however, and some claim that climate changes compelled Anishinabe relocation before European contact.[11]

According to their oral tradition (prior to their settlement of the Lake Superior area that included the northern homelands of Dakota people), Anishinabe people resided on the Atlantic Ocean near the Gulf of the St. Lawrence River. There they suffered misery and death and began following the Megis (seashell) westward until they finally arrived, centuries later, on the Island of LaPointe where the people settled.[12] La Pointe Island is located off the shore of northern Wisconsin in Lake Superior. Edward Benton Banai relates the message of their first prophet who said to the people, "In the time of the First Fire, the Anishinabe nation will rise up and follow the sacred shell of the Midewiwin Lodge. The Midewiwin Lodge will serve as a rallying point for the people and its traditional ways will be the source of much strength. The Sacred Megis will lead the way to the chosen ground of the Anishinabe. You are to look for a turtle shaped island that is linked to the purification of the earth. You will find such an island at the beginning and at the end of your journey. There will be seven stopping places along the way. You will know the chosen ground has been reached when you come to a land where food grows on water. If you do not move you will be destroyed."[13] The rice beds they found belonged to the Dakota Oyate. According to their oral tradition, then, the Anishinabe had a divine sanction to occupy what was Dakota homeland. Centuries of violence and animosity have consequently characterized relations between our two nations.

The areas in Minnesota typically associated with Anishinabe people today are those they took by force from Dakota people. According to early twentieth-century historian Newton Winchell's research, for example, in the time of Father Louis Hennepin's missionary and exploratory work among the Dakota (late seventeenth century), various Dakota bands were located as follows:

the Mdewakantunwan Dakota occupied the Mille Lacs region and the upper Rum River, Wahpetunwan Dakota at Sandy Lake north and west of Mille Lacs, the Sisitunwan Dakota north of Cass and Winnibegoshish lakes, the Ihanktunwan at Leech Lake, the Red River, and Pipestone, and the Titunwan around Big Stone Lake and Lake Traverse.[14] With the exceptions of the Pipestone, Big Stone Lake, and Lake Traverse village sites, every other site is now associated with the Anishinabe. Winchell also attributed the ancient mounds at Mille Lacs to the ancient "Sioux," citing the then "expert" opinion of Jacob V. Brower who had conducted an early archeological survey of the Mille Lacs site.[15]

Writers on the Dakota past have generally attributed the Dakota loss of our northern homeland to the weakening of our population to disease and the widespread acquisition of European arms by Anishinabe people prior to Dakota acquisition of European arms. Nineteenth-century missionary Samuel Pond, for instance, noted "The Ojibways obtained fire-arms sooner than the Dakotas, and therefore were able to drive them out of the wooded country about the sources of the Mississippi and Rum rivers. If they had come into possession of fire-arms as early as their enemies did, it is not probable that they would have lost any of their lands."[16]

Scholars frequently indicate the eagerness with which the Dakota embraced the fur trade, but this eagerness was at least, in part, an act necessary for survival.[17] In what would become an arms race among Indigenous populations, each Indigenous nation was drawn into the European market economy. By the late seventeenth century when the French established fur-trade relations, Anishinabe people had already moved into the Lake Superior area. This began an era of violent confrontations. Historian Roy Meyer suggests it was likely that the "Chippewas, moving westward along the south shore of Lake Superior and armed with firearms obtained through trade, developed expansionist ambitions similar to those displayed earlier by the Hurons and Ottawas."[18] However, regardless of whether the Anishinabe were interested in empire or simply acquiring adequate lands to ensure the survival of their people, the Dakota population suffered severe losses. European invasion and colonization of Indigenous lands throughout the continent had set into motion a chain of events that was eventually detrimental to all Indigenous Peoples.

Historians generally consider the well-known Battle of Kathio, estimated to have occurred between 1745 and 1750, to be one of the last major battles between the Anishinabe and the Dakota. It represented the final push of Dakota people out of our northern homeland. Anishinabe historian William Warren characterized the Anishinabe-Dakota relationship as that of "mortal enemies, waging against each other a bloody and exterminating warfare."[19] Warren, however, also relates examples of peaceful interactions over spans of several years in which Dakota and Anishinabe people visited each other's villages and married into each other's families.[20] Nonetheless, these periods of peace were short-lived and by the mid-eighteenth century hostilities escalated again culminating in a fierce battle at Mille Lacs.

Warren attributes Anishinabe success at Mille Lacs to "more deadly weaponry" and details an incident in which Ojibway warriors put small bundles of gun powder in the smoke-holes of Dakota homes: "Not having as yet, like the more fortunate Ojibways, been blessed with the presence of White traders, the Dakotas were still ignorant of the gunpowder." Thus, at the end of the three-day struggle, the Dakota people were "swept away for ever from their favorite village sites."[21] Some of the fleeing Dakota settled in a village along the Rum River for a period, but the Anishinabe drove them out, too, after the battle of Crow Wing in 1770. From that point forward, the Dakota people were permanently forced from this northern region.[22] According to the Mille Lacs Band of Ojibwe Web site, their ancestors arrived in the area about 1700, but no mention is made of battles with the Dakota.[23]

While Dakota people had engaged in some form of agriculture for centuries prior to Anishinabe and European invasion,

Dakota people relied heavily on wild rice and maple sugar as important food sources. While these could be obtained on a much smaller scale in southern Minnesota (patches of wild rice existed along small stretches of the Minnesota River, for example), the abundance with which those food sources were found in northern Minnesota could not be replicated. This meant the dramatic loss of subsistence for Dakota people that continues to the present day.

The United States government then codified and legalized the occupation of Dakota lands by Anishinabe people when they entered into treaties with the Anishinabe. Through treaties, the Anishinabe ceded and reserved for themselves parcels of Dakota homeland. The Anishinabe Treaty of 1837, for example, ceded much of the land north of the boundary articulated in an 1825 agreement (an agreement orchestrated by the United States government between the Anishinabe and Dakota). Governor Lewis Cass of Michigan and Governor William Clark of Missouri mediated the 1825 treaty on behalf of the United States. Through this agreement, the United States intended to create a territorial boundary between "Chippewa" and "Sioux" lands so that our two nations would refrain from intertribal warfare. This boundary, however, became the dividing line for future Anishinabe land cessions.

Despite its intent, the 1825 agreement was not successful in ensuring peace between the Dakota and Anishinabe, and violent relations continued. For example, Indian Agent Major Lawrence Taliaferro wrote to the Fort Snelling commander, Major Bliss, in 1835 that "the Chippewa would not observe the landmarks, but on the contrary had been throwing them down and attempting to demolish many of them." He believed violence would consequently erupt because their country was not sufficient for the population and they would, thus, force themselves onto Dakota hunting grounds.[24] Periodic violence persisted between the Anishinabe and the Dakota until 1862–63.

These tensions became secondary to the threat posed by

invading Whites, however, and a ruthlessly expansionist United States government. Land cessions, for both Indigenous nations, were soon wrested away using whatever means were necessary.

Wasicu Invasion

The hunger for Indigenous lands by the swelling American population cannot be overstated. In fact, as Minnesota history will demonstrate, Europeans and Euro-Americans would commit some of the most heinous crimes in human history to obtain Indigenous lands. Unfortunately, Minnesota history is not unique. Europeans and Americans perpetrated similar crimes against humanity from coast to coast upon hundreds of Indigenous nations.

By the mid-nineteenth century when Whites began flooding into what was first claimed by them as Northwest Territory (1797), then Wisconsin Territory (1836), and then Minnesota Territory (1849), they had already established a pattern of aggression and violence. Indian traders were the advance guard for an exploitative process that would not end until settler society had stripped Indigenous Peoples of nearly everything we held dear. Military forts, ultimately designed to protect White economic interests, followed the traders and they, in turn, provided a base of protection for the soldiers, missionaries, and thousands of predominantly White settlers who followed. Whites who came to Minnesota had no intention of living side by side with either Dakota or Anishinabe Peoples; rather they arrived believing that the "Indian problem" would be dispelled in short order. They also believed the risk-taking associated with their early arrival would be rewarded with the best and biggest parcels of land for the smallest cost.

The exceptions to this rule might be the traders whose business required them to often live amongst the "Indians" so they could better exploit them (and their actions were hardly benign), or the missionaries and Indian agents whose professions required their living in close proximity to the "savages" (about whom they professed to be concerned). However, even the missionaries and agents had no intention of living side by side with "savages" indefinitely. Instead, they intended to engage in a radical campaign to "civilize" and "Christianize" the "heathen red men." While many Americans tend to look fondly on the work of missionaries and do-gooders claiming to bring lightness to the corners of the world where all the dark-skinned people dwell, this is not how Indigenous Peoples usually perceive their efforts. We identify these practices not only as a form of fanatical religious imperialism, but also as a form of ethnocide.

Thus, we must be clear that there was nothing benign about the actions or the goals of those Americans and Europeans who arrived in Dakota homeland. On the contrary, the first populations to invade these lands did so with complete disregard for the welfare or humanity of the Peoples who already dwelt here. Americans simply wanted the land and they did not care what they would have to do to obtain it.

Legalized Land Theft

Treaties are peculiar documents in United States history. Theoretically, if nations negotiate an agreement and one side violates the terms of the treaty, that unilateral violation would render the treaty null and void, and conditions would return to their pre-treaty status.[25] This has not been the case, however, when the United States consistently violated their treaty obligations to Indigenous nations. Vine Deloria Jr. shocked the country when in 1969 he wrote in the midst of the Cold War, "America has yet to keep one Indian treaty or agreement despite the fact that the United States government signed over four hundred such treaties and agreements with Indian tribes. It would take Russia another century to make and break as many treaties as the United States has already violated."[26] Consequently, Indigenous nation after Indigenous nation has ceded lands and resources for promises the U.S. never fulfilled. Or, such fraudulent tactics were used to obtain Indigenous signatures that the treaties never should have been ratified. By the mid-nineteenth century, most of the treaties had simply become a form of legalized land theft. Nowhere is this more apparent than the treaties negotiated with the Dakota people of Minnesota.

The first Dakota land cession demonstrates the duplicitous nature of U.S. negotiations with our ancestors as well as the legal farce that would typify all subsequent treaties. In 1805, Zebulon Pike was commissioned by the federal government to negotiate a treaty for the purpose of establishing U.S. sovereignty in the region. Through the acquisition of Dakota lands, the Americans could build a military post, thereby challenging British influence and presence. Dakota people were caught in a contest between imperial powers, each intent on acquiring and exploiting Indigenous lands and resources for their own purposes. Pike feebly attempted to secure Dakota signatures to the treaty, but when he could only secure two, it did not stop him from proceeding as though the treaty had a measure of legitimacy (nor did it stop the Senate from later ratifying the treaty). At best, two signatures could represent only two villages and two of the Seven Council Fires of the Dakota Oyate (and it is more likely they were both from the Bdewakantunwan Council Fire). This was grossly inadequate for a treaty that was supposed to represent the will and agreement of the entire "Sioux" nation, which even Pike estimated to be 21,675.[27]

This treaty demonstrates that the U.S. government was not interested in fair negotiations, just that it could claim to have someone's signature on record agreeing to relinquish land. Moreover, at the end of the council, Pike provided 60 gallons of liquor to the Dakota men in attendance.[28] U.S. government negotiators frequently employed this method of enticement to achieve their desired aims in dealings with Indigenous Peoples. It helped them achieve the advantage in treaty negotiations by gaining the acquiescence of individuals they could lure with the promise of alcohol, or in some cases, by lubricating the deal-making at the start. In 1805, at the time of this treaty negotiation, Dakota people would have likely never experienced alcohol in that quantity before.

In addition, Pike never specified an amount for payment to the Dakota Oyate in the treaty, so when it was finally ratified in 1808, the Senate filled in the blank. They directed the U.S. government to pay only one hundredth of the amount initially estimated by Pike for acceptable payment. While $200 worth of gifts and alcohol were distributed at the treaty site to the two sig-natories, in the end, the United States claimed at least 100,000 acres of prime real estate in what is now the Twin Cities metro-politan area for the unconscionable price of $2,000, a mere two cents an acre. Even then, it was not until 1819 that the U.S. finally offered $2,000 in goods to the Dakota as belated payment.[29] This treaty set the tone for Dakota–U.S. relations and Dakota people have never forgotten the unethical means by which the United States initially took our lands.

By the nineteenth century, the U.S. government realized that it could not afford costly wars with every Indigenous nation. Yet, at the same time, its expansionist policies required somehow wresting control of Indigenous lands away from Indigenous Peoples. Europeans and Euro-Americans assumed when they invaded Indigenous lands that the United States government would eventually acquire those lands. For example, an 1849 map of southern Minnesota depicting potential railway lines indi-cates that long before the U.S. would negotiate the 1851 trea-ties (which eventually ceded those lands and confined Dakota people to reservations along the Minnesota River), it was as-sumed that Dakota people would be dispossessed from that land base. Americans obtained every square inch of land they now occupy at the expense of Indigenous Peoples. Similarly, Min-nesotans obtained every acre of Minnesota at the expense of Indigenous Peoples. Treaties became a means to avoid warfare, temporarily at least, while also gaining access to Dakota lands and resources.[30] The Treaty of 1805 exemplified that point and the United States continued to use rank means to secure Dakota lands. In future years, our people fared no better in succeeding treaty negotiations. The United States further divested us of our homeland in the treaties of 1830, 1837, 1851, and 1858. The most outrageous treaty examples, however, are the Treaties of Traverse des Sioux and Mendota negotiated in 1851.

1851 Treaties

In his chapter detailing these treaty negotiations, entitled "The Monstrous Conspiracy," historian Roy Meyer describes how Dakota leaders were alternately promised and threatened in order to secure signatures on treaties. He argues that these treaties are "equal in infamy to anything else in the long history of injustice perpetrated upon the Indians by the authorized representatives of the United States government in the name of that government."[31]

The Treaty of Traverse des Sioux (negotiated with the Sisitunwan and Wahpetunwan) and the Treaty of Mendota (negotiated with the Bdewakantunwan and the Wahpekute) ceded all remaining Dakota land claims, except a twenty-mile-long strip of land bordering the Minnesota River, from Lake Traverse to the Yellow Medicine for the "Upper Sioux," and from Yellow Medicine to the Little Rock stream for the "Lower Sioux."[32] Ultimately, to obtain the necessary signatures, U.S. treaty negotiators—including Commissioner of Indian Affairs Luke Lea and Minnesota Territorial Governor Alexander Ramsey—had to repeatedly threaten the Dakota with the withholding of rations (rations theoretically guaranteed from previous treaties) or threaten to take the land by force leaving the Dakota with no compensation. Lea went so far as to suggest that if they did not sign, the Great Father could come with 100,000 men and drive the Dakota to the Rocky Mountains.[33] Thus, fear of starvation and loss of lands by force compelled our Dakota leaders to sign the treaties.

1851 Traverse des Sioux Treaty "negotiations." *Painting by Francis Davis Millet. Courtesy of the Minnesota Historical Society.*

To compound the deceit, as leaders signed first the original treaty, then a copy, they were pulled by the blanket to a third table and pressured to sign what became known as the "trader's papers," documents the Dakota leaders could not read. These documents (in violation of the Act of 1847 that required that all moneys due Indians be paid to the heads of families or individuals) signed over moneys directly to traders in payment of alleged debts accrued by the Dakota. At the Treaty of Traverse des Sioux, trader Joseph Brown held the pen as the chiefs were encouraged to sign the paper that was never read or explained to them.[34] Even missionary Thomas Williamson believed it to be a triplicate copy of the treaty. After they realized what they had signed, Dakota leaders contested their validity, but the United States ultimately upheld them as legitimate.

Through the grossly inflated figures specified in the trader's papers, traders gained substantial wealth at Dakota expense. For example, just through the shenanigans associated with the Treaty of Traverse des Sioux, Henry Hastings Sibley was paid

$66,459 in one lump sum. This was in addition to the 10 per-
cent he deducted from the Wahpekute fund for acting as "attorney" in the Treaty of Mendota. This is how White opportunists
gained fortunes in Minnesota, through the exploitation of Dakota people at Dakota expense. In this same treaty, J. B. Fari-
bault was paid $22,500, Alexander Faribault was paid $13,500,
and twenty other traders, missionaries Williamson and Riggs,
and fifty "half-breeds" with their families also received a portion
of the trader's claims.[35] Thus, for ceding somewhere between
24,000,000 and 35,000,000 acres of rich agricultural lands, hundreds of thousands of dollars immediately went into the hands of
individual Whites.[36] Hugh Tyler, responsible for distributing the
treaty money, took $50,000 for his share and rumors abounded
regarding Ramsey's likely cut. What is certain is that White traders and lawyers profited far more than any Dakota people from
the 1851 treaties.

As disturbing as these trader's actions appear, however, they
are still no match for the level of duplicity demonstrated by Lea
and Ramsey acting as United States government officials. The financial terms of the treaties reveal the fantastic degrees to which
the United States would go to avoid providing fair compensation
to the Dakota. The details must have been utterly incomprehensible to Dakota people unschooled in Western economic practices and double-dealing.

Both treaties of 1851 outline a plan for payment of annuities
that included $1,665,000 for the "Upper Sioux" and $1,410,000
to the "Lower Sioux." The bulk of the money was to remain in
trust ($1,360,000 for the "Upper Sioux" and $1,160,000 for the
"Lower Sioux"), bearing an interest rate of 5 percent for fifty
years. The government was supposed to pay the interest on
the trust account annually to the Dakota so that Dakota people
would receive a constant source of money and supplies during
that fifty-year period. At first glance, readers might believe this
to be a wise financial strategy that would always ensure an annual
payment to the Dakota. However, according to these treaties, the

principal amount would not revert to the Dakota at the end of the fifty-year period.[37] Instead, the U.S. government would pay the Dakota off the interest and then keep the principal, never paying even the measly amount of thirteen cents an acre (almost nine cents an acre if the land cession is 35,000,000) offered for the 1851 land cessions. In the end, the government would keep the money and get the land![38] That means the government paid $690,000 for the land cession and the Dakota actually received not quite three cents an acre for 24,000,000 acres (or about two cents an acre if we use the 35,000,000-acre land cession). However, even that figure is not accurate because White Minnesotans immediately directed $370,000 to the traders and mixed-bloods rather than to the Dakota people who were supposed to be the beneficiaries of moneys from the land ceded.[39] With that figured into the computations, Americans, theoretically, would pay the Dakota about a penny an acre on this major land transaction.

When the treaty arrived in Washington, new debates emerged within the Senate. Consequently, the Senate barely passed it with amendments. The amendments were egregious, however, and entirely detrimental to the Dakota. The Senate struck the provisions guaranteeing the Dakota reservations, essentially leaving the Dakota landless by legal principles and wholly subject to the whim of the president. Instead of a legal title, the Senate authorized the president to select what he deemed a suitable site for a Dakota reservation for as long as he deemed necessary.[40] While the terms of the original treaty were in no way representative of just dealings with the Dakota, the Senate's striking of the land provision was more than callous; it was criminal. The appropriation bill for payment to the Dakota contained two provisos, however. The first one required that government officials obtain the assent of the Dakota to the amendments. The second required the money to go directly to the Dakota, "unless the imperious interest of the Indian or Indians, or some treaty stipulation, shall require the payment to be made otherwise, under the direction of the President."[41]

To obtain Dakota consent, White Minnesotans used various tactics ranging from violence and coercion to extortion and bribery to gain signatures indicating agreement to the Senate-amended treaties and the trader's claims. The Dakota went into the negotiations as cold weather loomed with limited food supplies, so it was no surprise that Ramsey used 1837 treaty annuities as a bargaining chip against the Bdewakantunwan, withholding the annuities until they concluded "negotiations." Ramsey also used bribery as a means to obtain signatures. For example, he told the Dakota that if they signed the amendments, he would make sure that soldiers would finally release five imprisoned Dakota warriors held at Fort Snelling.

However, historian William Folwell attributes Ramsey's most effective "negotiating" tactic to his divide and conquer strategy. By making separate distributions of gold to individual leaders, Ramsey was able to pit the chiefs against one another and play on their individual fears. By negotiating with them individually, Ramsey could convince them that if they did not sign, they would be left with no money while the other chiefs who did sign would receive their share. Ramsey divided twenty thousand dollars among seven Bdewakantunwan chiefs, and Wabasha and Wacouta were the first to accept the gold at a late-night private meeting with Ramsey. The other chiefs then followed suit.

Yet, even after the Bdewakantunwan signed the new papers, the "Upper" Dakota continued to contest the terms. To silence one of the leaders of the opposition and thereby diminish the organized protest, Ramsey incarcerated chief Red Iron until after he obtained the necessary signatures.[42] Even then, he had to resort to bringing in chiefs singly or in pairs and handing out annuities to them if they would sign privately. He then added the date to the document with their signatures, as if they all signed together in formal council.[43]

In the end, Whites flooded into Dakota homeland under the banner of treaties that undoubtedly represent some of the most outrageous and fraudulent examples in American history. Even then, the United States government did not keep these deplorable treaty terms. Repeated violations included skipped or delayed treaty payments, unrealized terms directing educational or agricultural funds for the Dakota, and a constant influx of White settlers on Dakota lands, both before and after ratification. The treaties of 1851 were not the last ones the United States negotiated with Dakota people, nor were they the only ones secured by fraudulent means. The United States "negotiated" another set of treaties in 1858 using similarly deceitful methods and faulty premises. They exemplify both the gross power imbalance existing in favor of the United States over Dakota people as well as the total disregard for fair dealings exhibited by the United States.

While the United States negotiation of the treaties and their unfulfilled terms are shameful, they represent only the beginning phases of White crimes against Dakota people that would grow increasingly violent and inhumane. At this point in the historical narrative, it is appropriate to shift to another framework for examining what followed: the United Nations Convention on Prevention and Punishment of the Crime of Genocide.

International Standards for Genocide

The UN Convention details agreed upon international standards for determining what constitutes genocide in Article II, which states: "In the present Convention, genocide means any of the following acts committed with intent to destroy, in whole or in part, a national, ethnical, racial or religious group, as such:

(a) Killing members of the group;
(b) Causing serious bodily or mental harm to members of the group;
(c) Deliberately inflicting on the group conditions of life calculated to bring about its physical destruction in whole or in part;

(d) Imposing measures intended to prevent births within
the group;

(e) Forcibly transferring children of the group to another
group."[44]

I must emphasize that any one of these criteria met singly constitutes genocide. In the nineteenth and twentieth centuries,
however, the United States government and its citizens violated
all of these criteria in multiple ways. Certainly, Whites in Minnesota perpetrated these crimes. This next section will highlight
examples in each of the categories to demonstrate how genocide
was committed in Dakota homeland against Dakota people.

Criterion A

Criterion "(a) Killing members of the group" is most apparent
in the actions of White Minnesotans during events surrounding the forced expulsion of Dakota people from our homeland.
Many Minnesotans are familiar with the U.S.–Dakota War of
1862 (previously referred to as the "Sioux Uprising" or "Dakota
Conflict") and understand that the war did not begin because of
a single wrong perpetrated by White settlers. Rather most people
familiar with the history understand that war was declared
by Dakota warriors as a last desperate attempt to save Dakota
homeland and way of life from White invasion and conquest, or
to die trying in what appeared to many of them as a futile effort.
Dakota people initiated the war in response to treaty violations
and the accompanying violence originating from White invasion
and colonization. Yet, White Minnesotans were able to use the
U.S.–Dakota War of 1862 as their justification for complete land
theft and an extraordinarily successful policy of genocide and
ethnic cleansing. White Minnesotans carried out many of the
events that followed with the ultimate aim of eliminating Dakota
presence from the state of Minnesota, in one way or another.

For example, on September 9, 1862, Governor Alexander

Alexander Ramsey, architect of Minnesota's policy of Dakota extermination and forced removal. *Courtesy of the Minnesota Historical Society.*

Ramsey declared before the Minnesota state legislature "The Sioux Indians of Minnesota must be exterminated or driven forever beyond the borders of the State."[45] This was an unambiguous directive in 1862 and it remains a clearly and concisely stated genocidal decree today. Ramsey's statement provides the first element required in defining genocide, and that is the aspect of intent. Boldly stated, there is no question about Ramsey's interest in destroying Dakota people, and the physical acts that followed his directive fulfill the physical element required in determining genocide, particularly under the first criteria. Furthermore, the events that followed in Minnesota make the most sense in the context of Ramsey's declaration. That is, he provided the genocidal ideology that drove White actions in the aftermath of the war.

Upon the defeat suffered by Dakota people militarily, many Dakota people fled westward or northward in hopes of escaping what they suspected would be inhumane treatment by the United States military and citizenry. While Dakota men, in particular, lost their lives during the war, most of the purposeful killing of Dakota people occurred after the war had ended and when Dakota people offered little threat to White settlement. Military conquest of the Dakota was not enough to satisfy the aims of Governor Ramsey, however, who responded with relish to the appeals for mass killings shouted by Minnesota's citizenry.

At the end of the war, when the surrendered or captured

Dakota people remained, General Henry Hastings Sibley and his soldiers immediately separated the Dakota men from the women and children. The men allowed for this separation voluntarily after soldiers told them that for payment of their overdue treaty annuities, the men would need to be counted.[46] Believing the lie espoused by Sibley and his men, Dakota warriors were disarmed, shackled, and subjected to outrageous trials before a military tribunal composed of White Minnesotans.

The five-man tribunal eventually sentenced over three hundred Dakota men to death by hanging and another sixteen to prison terms. This was an attempt to execute immediately over 15 percent of the surrendered Dakota population. Since this group was composed of the able-bodied resisters to American invasion and land theft, if fully carried out, Minnesotans would have largely eliminated the capacity for Dakota reproduction and resistance. A population cannot survive long without its able-bodied male population.

In the end, President Abraham Lincoln ordered the execution of thirty-nine of those men and pardoned one more at the last minute, killing thirty-eight Dakota martyrs in what remains the largest mass execution in United States history. The hanging occurred the day after Christmas, on December 26, 1862. This mass hanging was such a phenomenon that at one time it earned a place in the *Guinness Book of World Records* for the largest simultaneous mass hanging from one gallows.[47]

Several years after the 1862 war, when Dakota warriors were still imprisoned and Dakota people had no capacity to threaten White Minnesotans, White soldiers hanged two more Dakota leaders. Leaders Sakpe and Medicine Bottle had fled to Canada for safety at the end of the 1862 war, but it did not stop Whites from pursuing their capture and execution. Because they remained on the other side of the border, however, White soldiers had to use illegal and foul means to secure their arrest. Canadian officials, Captain John H. McKenzie of Fort Garry, Onisime Giguere, and Andrew Bannatyne, drugged Sakpe and

Thirty-eight Dakota men lynched at Mankato, December 26, 1862. *Painting by W. H. Childs. Courtesy of the Minnesota Historical Society.*

Medicine Bottle with wine spiked with laudanum and then tied a chloroform-saturated handkerchief over Sakpe's face. They then bound both Medicine Bottle and Sakpe, tied them to sleds, and delivered them into the hands of American Major Edwin Hatch at Pembina in Dakota Territory. White soldiers next set up a military tribunal similar to the previous one and put Medicine Bottle and Sakpe on trial. The makeshift tribunal issued judgments of execution against the two leaders in late 1864, but it took nearly a year before President Andrew Johnson confirmed the execution order and White Minnesotans could finally implement it. On November 11, 1865, White soldiers executed Sakpe and Medicine Bottle by hanging at Fort Snelling.[48]

These were not the only deaths suffered by Dakota people, however. Settler society perpetrated numerous killings, not only through direct violence, but also through the forced removals and incarceration of Dakota people without providing adequate food, clothing, shelter, and protection. Populations simply cannot survive without adequate provisions. The resulting deaths

Fort Snelling concentration camp, 1862. *Photo by Benjamin Franklin Upton. Courtesy of the Minnesota Historical Society.*

are therefore killings, rather than inevitable or unpreventable consequences. Nowhere is this clearer than in the forced removals and concentration camp imprisonment of Dakota people during the winter of 1862–63.

After the surrender and capture of Dakota people in the fall of 1862, Sibley and his men instituted a severe system of gender segregation. They dealt with the men in one group and the women and children in another. As already mentioned, White soldiers singled out and subjected Dakota men to military tribunals. Then, while the men were awaiting President Lincoln's execution orders, soldiers first kept them at Lower Sioux and then forcibly removed them to a concentration camp in Mankato. On November 8, 1862, Dakota men, shackled two by two, were loaded onto wagons and they began their painful journey to Mankato. White mobs assaulted them, throwing rocks, sticks, and brickbats at them, and wielding bullwhips and pitchforks against them until they were bloody and beaten. One soldier guarding a wagon commented that eight out of the ten Indians he was guarding in his wagon were hurt as they went through New Ulm, some sustaining mortal wounds.[49] It did not matter that these men were unarmed. Even White children felt that those Dakota men deserved whatever horrors could be meted out against them because they had dared to attack White settlers. In 1862, White settlers could understand wanting to kill the people attacking them in their homes and towns, but they could not see the similarities with the Dakota defense of our homeland. Indeed, they considered Dakota use of violence in defense of homeland as savage. They felt they had a superior right to Dakota homeland, because they were, well, superior and White.

Minnesotans treated Dakota women and children in a similar fashion. Soldiers paraded them through White towns as well, as they made their way to the concentration camp at Fort Snelling. Most of the Dakota women and children walked, however. Only small numbers rode on carts reserved for the very elderly and the very young. Furthermore, this population was experiencing a widespread epidemic of measles with symptoms such as a rash, fever, cough, red and watery eyes, vomiting, diarrhea, ear infections and pneumonia. This epidemic would likely have affected about 85 percent of the women and children, all while they were force-marched over twenty miles a day.[50] In addition to accounts of sickness, Dakota families carry oral accounts detailing assaults by both White soldiers and citizens alike. For example, we have Dakota stories about White soldiers stabbing and shooting elderly grandmothers as well as stories of brutal assaults by White townspeople. One of the more horrific details remembered among the descendants of those who survived the death marches involves White townspeople pouring hot, scalding water on the elderly women and children who were riding in carts as they traveled through New Ulm. Torture and killings were the norm along this route rather than the exception. To this day, Dakota people do not know what happened to the bodies of our ancestors murdered by White Minnesotans on this forced death march.

Unfortunately, the deaths continued during the winter of 1862–63 as White Minnesotans intentionally imprisoned Dakota people without adequate food, shelter, clothing, or protection.

On November 27, 1862, a girl from Red Wing, for example, reported about Fort Snelling, "There are a few squaws killed up at the fort every week . . . always cut their throats by running against a knife. The Third [Regiment] buries them in a hole, face downwards."[51] White soldiers could routinely perpetrate sexual violence against Dakota women and girls and then simply dispose of their bodies. Moreover, they could do so without fear of retributive violence from male Dakota relatives who were helpless to defend their women and children because they were imprisoned elsewhere.[52]

Other deaths occurred from the epidemics still spreading through the Fort Snelling concentration camp. In reference to Dakota arrival at Fort Snelling, Gabriel Renville commented, "We all moved into this inclosure, but we were so crowded and confined that an epidemic broke out among us and the children were dying day and night."[53] In late January 1863, Stephen Riggs wrote to his brother, "It is a very sad place now. The crying

Dakota women imprisoned
at Fort Snelling, 1862–63.
Photo by Rodolph W. Ransom.
Courtesy of the Minnesota
Historical Society.

Apistoka, Fort Snelling concentration camp, 1862–63. *Photo by Benjamin Franklin Upton. Courtesy of the Minnesota Historical Society.*

hardly ever stops. From five to ten die daily." Good Star Woman related, "Sometime 20 to 50 died in one day and were buried in a long trench, the old, large people underneath and the children on top."[54] Others were so sick with grief that they no longer wanted to live. Wabasha's wife, for example, literally starved herself out of a sense of grief she experienced over the hanging of her brother, White Dog, at Mankato.[55]

Ironically, in the twenty-first century some writers of history still maintain the perverted colonialist perception of these events. Corinne Monjeau-Marz, for example, rejects the term concentration camp as an accurate identifier. Instead, she considers Fort Snelling a site of Dakota preservation stating, "in post-war Minnesota, this option helped preserve them." This perspective completely denies and renders benign the violent and brutal processes of invasion, conquest, and ethnic cleansing that accompanied White "settlement." In reality, Dakota people would have been well preserved without Fort Snelling if White

Fort Snelling
Concentration Camp,
1862–63.
Whitney's Gallery.
Courtesy of the Minnesota
Historical Society.

people simply stopped making false promises, invading, stealing, and desecrating Dakota lands and resources, and killing Dakota people. To put it clearly, if they left Dakota homeland, White Minnesotans would not have to imprison Dakota people in concentration camps. It is precisely because White Minnesotans wanted to continue their occupation of Dakota homeland that Dakota populations were threatened. Fort Snelling did not protect Dakota people. Rather, it served to concentrate and subjugate our population as Minnesotans prepared to remove us from our homeland.

In spring 1863, the stage was set for White Minnesotans to launch a full-scale campaign of ethnic cleansing, thus helping to fulfill Governor Ramsey's call for extermination or forced removal. Minnesota's soldiers forced the remaining populations on boats that went down the Mississippi River. The condemned men (those the soldiers did not hang in Mankato) were imprisoned in Davenport, Iowa. The military escorted the women and children to a new concentration camp site in Crow Creek,

Little Crow.
*Photo by Joel
Emmons Whitney.
Courtesy of
the Minnesota
Historical Society.*

$500 bounty payment for the murder of Little Crow. *Courtesy of the
Minnesota Historical Society.*

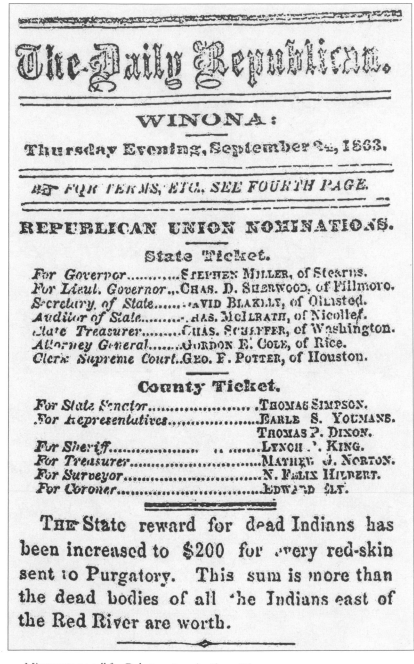

The Daily Republican.

WINONA:

Thursday Evening, September 24, 1863.

FOR TERMS, ETC., SEE FOURTH PAGE.

REPUBLICAN UNION NOMINATIONS.

State Ticket.

For Governor.............STEPHEN MILLER, of Stearns.
For Lieut. Governor...CHAS. D. SHERWOOD, of Fillmore.
Secretary of State.......DAVID BLAKELY, of Olmsted.
Auditor of State...........HAS. McILRATH, of Nicollet.
State Treasurer..........CHAS. SCHEFFER, of Washington.
Attorney General.......GORDON E. COLE, of Rice.
Clerk Supreme Court..GEO. F. POTTER, of Houston.

County Ticket.

For State Senator.......................THOMAS SIMPSON.
For Representatives..................EARLE S. YOUMANS.
                                          THOMAS P. DIXON.
For Sheriff..................... ....LYNCH .'. KING.
For Treasurer.............................MATHEW J. NORTON.
For Surveyor...............................N. FELIX HILBERT.
For Coroner...............................EDWARD SLY.

THE State reward for dead Indians has been increased to $200 for every red-skin sent to Purgatory. This sum is more than the dead bodies of all the Indians east of the Red River are worth.

Minnesotans call for Dakota extermination, 1863.
Image courtesy of Chris Mato Nunpa.

South Dakota (via the Mississippi and Missouri Rivers). Conditions were no better for the men in Davenport or the women and children at Crow Creek than they were in the previous concentration camps.

But, let us return to the UN Genocide Convention. There are still more examples that meet criterion "(a) Killing members of the group." Once Minnesotans achieved the forced removal of Dakota people out of Minnesota, Ramsey ordered punitive expeditions into Dakota Territory to hunt down Dakota people in flight. While Sibley's enemies saw the 1863 expeditions as ineffectual because the soldiers were unable to kill or capture large numbers of Indians, the expeditions were incredibly harmful to Dakota people. In addition to causing terror, the expeditions destroyed vast quantities of Dakota supplies and equipment. Thus, the victories were one-sided in favor of White interests. The battles primarily consisted of Dakota warriors trying desperately to fend off White soldiers while their women and children fled behind them.[56] Of course, most of the casualties of these expeditions would occur the following winter when the Dakota populations on the run starved or died of exposure.

Still, that was not enough to satisfy the quest for total annihilation. Minnesotans placed bounties on the scalps of Dakota people beginning in the summer of 1863. They began at twenty-five dollars and eventually reached two hundred dollars. Though bounties on human beings were illegal at the time, even according to United States laws, it did not prevent White Minnesotans from enacting the bounty system and awarding money to beneficiaries.[57] For example, Winona's newspaper, *The Daily Republican*, issued the call for bounties on September 23, 1863, stating, "The State reward for dead Indians has been increased to $200 for every red-skin sent to Purgatory. The sum is more than the dead bodies of all the Indians east of the Red River are worth." White Minnesotans were clamoring for complete extermination or removal, the state government was obliging with public policy, and the media was encouraging indiscriminant Indian killing. This undoubtedly meets several of the criteria set out in the Genocide Convention.

Criterion B

The second criterion is "(b) Causing serious bodily or mental harm to members of the group." Bodily harm in this case may be more easily determined and includes all the examples cited above in which Whites killed Dakota people, as well as all the instances in which Dakota people suffered physical trauma short of death. These would include such examples as those who suffered beatings, whippings, and scalding water on the forced marches; those who suffered sickness and exposure because of inadequate shelter; those who suffered starvation as White soldiers hunted them down; and the women who suffered sexual assault while under government confinement.

Mental harm, however, is not readily apparent to settler society because in many instances settlers still believe in the superiority of their ways of being and living. From that perspective,

Pipestone Indian School, an institution of colonialism.
Courtesy of the Minnesota Historical Society.

Children at Pipestone, 1893. *Courtesy of the Minnesota Historical Society.*

settler society might even view colonization as beneficial to Indigenous Peoples. However, perpetrators in this context are not morally positioned to make the determination of mental harm for Indigenous Peoples. Rather, only the victims can determine if they have suffered mental harm. Obviously mental harm accompanies bodily harm, but there are additional circumstances that also warrant consideration under this criterion. I would argue that the processes of invasion, conquest, and colonization also fit under this criterion because of the severe psychological harms that consequently occurred to the Dakota psyche. What kind of mental harm is perpetrated against a people's leadership when the more powerful nation is not fulfilling its treaty obligations? What kind of mental harm is perpetrated upon a people overwhelmed by hopelessness and powerlessness because they have no effective way to defend their lands and people from an outside threat? What kind of mental harm is done to a people dispossessed of their homeland?

These harms did not end in the nineteenth century. One of

the federally mandated boarding schools located in Minnesota, for example, was Pipestone Indian School. The purpose of federal boarding schools was to perpetrate ethnocide. While the UN Convention on Genocide does not specify ethnocide as genocide, the effects of ethnocide upon the victims certainly constitute mental harm.[58] Within the federal boarding schools, the general policy was "Kill the Indian, Save the Man." School officials implemented systematic efforts to strip away all traces of Indigeneity (including language, dress, long hair, spirituality, diet, worldview, economy, political and kinship systems, and of course, attachment to the land), while supplanting those ways with White, Christian values, worldview, and ways of being.

What makes this particular policy of ethnocide so heinous is that the U.S. government perpetrated this crime against the children, the most vulnerable segment of the Indigenous population. The confusion, self-hatred, identity conflicts, and trauma were so detrimental to the children who attended boarding schools that we still experience the disturbing effects in our communities today. Furthermore, the abuses at the boarding schools surpassed mental harms. They also included bodily harm through extreme forms of corporal punishment as well as physical and sexual abuse.[59] Certainly, the ethnocide that accompanied missionary efforts and boarding schools were violent and harmful enough to constitute genocide according to this particular criterion in the UN Genocide Convention.

In Minnesota, the government usually sent Dakota children to Pipestone Indian School, located in the southwestern portion of the state near the South Dakota border. Pipestone's buildings were erected in 1892 and doors opened to students the following year. The school remained in operation until 1953 when it was finally closed, affecting not just a single generation, but multiple generations of Dakota families. Many children entered the boarding schools when they were very young (five or six years of age). They consequently experienced years of indoctrination in anti-Indian ideology and frequently experienced a range of abuses perpetrated against them. As historian Andrea Smith points out, "Some colonists supported boarding schools because they thought cultural genocide was more cost-effective than physical genocide."[60] Though federally mandated boarding schools were characterized as part of U.S. policies of Indian assimilation, that presentation is much too benign. It would be much more accurate to describe the ethnocidal institutions as part of U.S. policies of brutal colonization and genocide.

Criterion C

The third criterion in the UN Genocide Convention, "(c) Deliberately inflicting on the group conditions of life calculated to bring about its physical destruction in whole or part," also applies to the Dakota experience in Minnesota. By the 1860s, the U.S. government had already removed hundreds of thousands of Indigenous Peoples from their homelands because citizens and all levels of government were intent upon wresting Indigenous lands away from Indigenous Peoples. Ethnic cleansing became a means to not only dispossess Indigenous Peoples, but also to eliminate the populations that would continue to contest or threaten the new White landlords.

Thomas Jefferson, for example, rigorously advocated for the extermination of Indigenous Peoples, stating, in 1807, "And . . . if we are constrained to lift the hatchet against any tribe, we will never lay it down till that tribe is exterminated, or is driven beyond the Mississippi . . . in war, they will kill some of us; we shall destroy all of them." Similarly, in 1813 Jefferson wrote, "that the American government has no other choice before it than to pursue [the Indians] to extermination, or drive them to new seats beyond our reach."[61] When Governor Ramsey made his similar declaration in 1862, he was merely following a tradition laid out previously by America's founding fathers. Jefferson was certainly the most articulate brainchild of the extraordinarily successful policies of forced removal that would become codified and executed under future presidential administrations.

The administration of Andrew Jackson in the 1830s, for example, was responsible for the forced march of the Tsalagi (Cherokee) on their Trail of Tears. This is perhaps the best-known forced march in American history, causing the deaths of approximately 8,000 of 17,000 Tsalagi men, women, and children because of their death march to Indian Territory.[62]

Sociologist Russell Thornton has documented losses for Indigenous Peoples due to genocide, and he comments that many, if not most, Indigenous Peoples were "removed, relocated, dispersed, concentrated, or forced to migrate at least once." He further states, "Both the concentration of American Indians in small geographic areas and the dispersal of them from their homelands caused increased mortality in Indian populations, typically because of associated military actions, disease, starvation, extremely harsh conditions during the moves, and the resulting destruction of ways of life."[63] Historian David Stannard agrees with Thornton regarding the widespread implementation of forced removals. He asserts, "The story of the southeastern Indians, like that of the northeastern tribes, was repeated across the entire expanse of the North American continent, as far south as Mexico, as far north as Canada and the Arctic, as far west as the coasts of Washington, Oregon, and California."[64]

The congregating of Dakota people in concentration camps and the ethnic cleansing of Dakota people out of Minnesota, therefore, fit into a long history of American brutality. Consequently, the deaths that occurred because of these policies would have been both foreseen and disregarded. It was certainly no secret to the U.S. government, state governments, or to White citizens that Indigenous people died during such brutal and traumatic experiences. Yet, the U.S. government and American citizens repeatedly and systematically continued to carry out policies of removal. They did not simply consider Dakota people

Attack on unarmed Dakota men, New Ulm, November 1862. *Harper's Weekly.*

expendable and appropriate targets of violent crimes; Dakota deaths provided an added bonus. With Dakota deaths, White citizens could get Indigenous land without fearing Indigenous retribution. Because many Whites would have preferred total extermination, they would have considered deaths from concentration camps or forced removals as beneficial.

In 1863, the legislation for Dakota ethnic cleansing was entitled "An Act for the Removal of the Sisseton, Wahpaton, Medwakanton, and Wahpakoota Bands of Sioux or Dakota Indians, and for the disposition of their Lands in Minnesota and Dakota." Tellingly, it accompanied another bit of legislation entitled "An Act for the Relief of Persons for Damages sustained by Reason of Depredations and Injuries by certain Bands of Sioux Indians."[65] These acts allowed for the unilateral abrogation of Dakota treaties, for the release of Dakota treaty annuities to White settlers in Minnesota, and for the U.S. military to implement a policy of ethnic cleansing. Because Dakota forced removal was legislated, we must consider the resulting deaths associated with the implementation of that legislation as deliberate. Furthermore, we must also consider as deliberate the deaths caused by the horrendous concentration camp conditions at Lower Sioux,

Mankato, Fort Snelling, Fort McClellan (Davenport), and Fort Thompson (Crow Creek). Imprisonment was no accident. It was a callous and inhumane government and citizenry that continued to subject Dakota people to long-term confinement while our people were dying. Yet, they continued to deny our Dakota ancestors their freedom.

Because the U.S. government repeated forced removals across the continent, by the 1860s it was clear that when they denied Indigenous Peoples their homelands and their ways of life, Indigenous Peoples tended to die in unusually high numbers. This was certainly true of the Dakota people, who began to die in unprecedented numbers when denied access to our traditional homeland. More than a third of the population, or 120 men, confined at Davenport (Fort McClellan) died during their three-year incarceration. Similarly, at the Crow Creek concentration camp in South Dakota where the women, children, and "friendlies" were confined, the death toll was extreme. Children frequently suffered the most as the death toll affected young people more dramatically. The missionary John P. Williamson wrote about the forced exile and the subsequent deaths, capturing the impact on the population:

> When 1300 Indians were crowded like slaves on the boiler and hurricane decks of a single boat, and fed on musty hardtack and briny pork, which they had not half a chance to cook, diseases were bred which made fearful havoc during the hot months, and the 1300 souls that were landed at Crow Creek June 1, 1863, decreased to one thousand. . . . So were the hills soon covered with graves.[66]

Other factors also affected birth and death rates among Dakota people. Thornton states that because of contact with Europeans, Indigenous People generally experienced diminished fecundity (ability to reproduce) and decreased fertility. While the influx of diseases certainly contributed to decreased fertility, so too did alcohol use as well as "warfare, genocide, removals, relocations, and destructions of ways of life."[67] Furthermore, at the same time that many factors were contributing to decreased fertility, mortality rates were also increasing.

Criterion D

In addition to the factors above contributing to a decreasing Dakota population, the United States government, the state of Minnesota, and White citizenry all helped ensure an additional reduction in population through the forced gender segregation occurring at the various concentration camp sites. This practice of separating out the women and children from the able-bodied men meets criterion (d) of the Genocide Convention, "Imposing measures intended to prevent births within the group." A population cannot possibly reproduce when the government disallows sexual relations between men and women. That is precisely what happened in the 1860s in conjunction with Minnesota's ethnic cleansing policies.

In the 1860s, Dakota people were experiencing enforced subfecundity (a diminished ability to reproduce) as a direct consequence of gender segregation. Furthermore, this segregation went on for prolonged periods. Considering that Dakota men were initially shackled and separated from their families by fall 1862, over a third of them were killed, and the rest of the imprisoned men were not released until spring 1866, it meant nearly four years of separation. This was devastating to the Dakota population at Crow Creek. Their population continued to decline while the United States government kept the men incarcerated. Furthermore, many of the births that did occur during that time would have been children born of the rape of Dakota women by White soldiers.

Unfortunately, in the twenty-first century, Dakota people continue to suffer disproportionately higher rates of incarceration than Whites. This means that enforced gender segregation is still negatively affecting the fecundity rates. We must remember that prior to colonization, Dakota people never experienced incarceration. We had a system of justice that allowed for the healing of harms without prisons. Indigenous people in prisons, therefore, are just another manifestation of colonialism at work in the United States, one with dire consequences for our people.

The United States has a poor track record in terms of violations against Indigenous women and our capacity for reproduction. One of the most flagrant violations of the UN Genocide Convention in this area involves the involuntary sterilization of Indigenous women in the late twentieth century. Various scholars have documented aspects of this 100 percent federally funded program administered to Indigenous Peoples through Indian Health Service (IHS) Hospitals as part of the Department of Health, Education and Welfare programs. We have yet to realize, however, the full extent of harm perpetrated under IHS. For example, in 1979 the General Accounting Office released a report based on a study of only four out of twelve IHS service areas (Albuquerque, Phoenix, Aberdeen, Oklahoma City), but that report was damaging enough to indicate a widespread genocidal practice. Within those four service areas, IHS sterilized 3,001 Indigenous women of childbearing age between 1973 and 1976, representing 5 percent of Indigenous women of childbearing age in those areas. Other surveys suggest that the practice of involuntary sterilization was much more widespread, with rates that ranged from 25 percent in the Oklahoma City area to 80 percent on other reservations.[68]

Many of the Dakota people living in exile, including those living on the Crow Creek, Lake Traverse, and Spirit Lake reservations, would have received healthcare within the Aberdeen service area, a known site of Indigenous involuntary sterilization practices. The same would be presumably true of the Indian Health Service facilities serving the Minnesota Dakota (as well as Anishinabe, Ho-Chunk, and other Indigenous populations in the region). We still need to investigate this matter further to disclose the truth regarding the full extent of involuntary sterilization practices, because current studies have only begun to skim the surface.

Furthermore, we have yet to learn the role of facilities such as the hospital built at the Pipestone Indian Training School that was completed in 1932. If sterilizations were performed at other government administered and funded institutions, it is not unreasonable to wonder what might have happened to Indigenous children while attending the boarding school at Pipestone with a hospital facility on the campus. What is certain is that the documented practice of involuntary sterilization was widely performed in the United States. According to international standards, this clearly constitutes genocide.

Criterion E

The last criterion (e) delineated in the UN Genocide Convention involves "Forcibly transferring children of the group to another group." The federally mandated boarding schools qualify under this criterion, as the government took Indigenous children away from their families of birth and delivered them into the hands of predominantly White, government-run institutions. Further, while the staff had the children away from the influence of their families and communities, they worked to destroy Indigenous ways of being. These institutions consequently caused irreparable harm to whole generations of children who grew up without Indigenous parenting skills. To make matters worse, the institutional staff often initiated vulnerable students into cycles of abusive behavior. Upon leaving the schools, students then carried those behaviors with them into their own families and communities.

This is not the only example of genocide that would fall under this criterion, however. Throughout the twentieth century, government officials took Indigenous children from their birth families in other ways as well. They abducted children for placement in White homes with White families. The dominant society frequently believed Indigenous families were inadequate in some way. Reasons for removing children were sometimes clear in terms of a record of violence or abuse. In other instances, however, the government removed children because their birth family was considered to be too poor, without the appropriate "necessities of civilization" such as indoor plumbing and electricity, or because their home was considered to have too many extended family members inhabiting it. Through foster and adoption care programs, the government placed Indigenous children in White homes, sometimes loving, sometimes not, so that they would theoretically "benefit" from the influences of "civilization." Historian Andrea Smith has written, "In Minnesota, Indian children were 500 percent more likely to be in foster care or adoptive care than non-Indian children" and "in South Dakota, Indian children were 1,600 percent more likely to be in foster or adoptive care."[69]

Loss of Indigenous children occurred unhindered until the passing of the Indian Child Welfare Act in 1978, and while that has slowed the flow of adoptions out of Indigenous communities, it has not halted it completely. Through such policies, the government has devastated Dakota children, families, and whole communities. Consequently, some of our people have been permanently lost from us.

This is of such widespread concern to Indigenous Peoples throughout the United States that Indigenous communities are now inventing new ways to attempt to self-heal communities and reconnect with one another. In October 2007, the White Earth Reservation sponsored a homecoming gathering for their Anishinabe people who had been adopted out.[70] It was, perhaps, the first of its kind in the United States, but it indicates the sense of loss and grief from a tremendous harm that has not yet been satisfactorily resolved.

Consequences of Genocide

This chapter has only briefly touched on a few of the examples of genocide perpetrated against Dakota people by White Americans, primarily so they could continue to occupy Dakota land unhindered. If we delve deeper into the historical record, we would find many more examples of other crimes against humanity and human injustices perpetrated for a variety of reasons. Furthermore, the crimes done to Dakota homeland, which I have not yet detailed here, are so extensive as to warrant the term *ecocide*. That is another category of harm that has deep and severe implications for the well-being of the planet and for Dakota people. Minnesotans and Americans need to address those harms as well.

Perhaps the clearest indication of the extent of harm caused by Minnesota's policy of ethnic cleansing is the lack of Dakota presence in Dakota homeland. We can see the evidence both in terms of Dakota land base and Dakota population. Before invasion and ethnic cleansing, Dakota land base would have included approximately 54,017,532 acres. Now Dakota people occupy about .006 percent of our original land base. Similarly, the population of Dakota people in Minnesota remains disproportionately small in the twenty-first century. According to the 2000 Census (including self-identified Dakota people among both reservation and urban populations), about 5,300 people claiming Dakota blood reside in the state. The 2003 Northwest Area Foundation statistics indicate that 2,265 of those individuals are citizens of the four federally recognized Dakota communities in Minnesota.[71] Meanwhile, contemporary data identifying Dakota populations in the United States and Canada is difficult to assess, in part because census materials do not always differentiate between Dakota, Lakota, and Nakota people. Self-identifiers as well as census officials maintain the use of the term "Sioux," making precision impossible. Thus, the "Sioux" population is calculated in the 2000 U.S. Census to be 167,869, with a portion of that being Dakota.[72] Many thousands more Dakota people still reside in Canada.

Because of the Dakota diaspora, most of our nation is still born into exile hundreds of miles away from our beautiful homeland.

We cannot relegate this reality to the depths of a single historical event or period in history. Instead, every generation of Dakota people has experienced this injustice since 1862. The injustice continues through the present day along with the other devastating consequences of living as colonized peoples. We continue to bear witness to the destruction of our homeland and to advocate for its survival. Settler society continues to deny us access to our sacred sites as well as the protection of our sacred sites. Settler society also continues to deny us access to many of the subsistence practices within the borders of *Minisota*. Our populations continue to face oppression in the existing educational, social welfare, economic, and criminal (in)justice institutions governing these lands. Our people continue to experience disproportionately high rates of early mortality, disease, suicide, depression, incarceration, chemical dependency, and violence. We are still suffering. While we need to do our part to recover healthy and sustainable ways of being, those recovery efforts will be futile if settler society continues to deny the inherent rights of Indigenous Peoples.

Notes

1. Because I am recounting this story from memory and Dale Childs is no longer available to verify this version, I apologize to him and to my elders for any errors in the story.

2. Dakota lands at one time would have at least included parts of what are now Wisconsin, Iowa, North Dakota, South Dakota, and Manitoba, Canada. Other scholars and tribal historians have argued that Dakota territory extended as far as Saskatchewan, Alberta, Montana, Wyoming, Nebraska, Colorado, Kansas, Missouri, Arkansas, and Illinois. Leo Omani from the Wahpeton Reserve near Prince Albert, Saskatchewan, for example, cites the work of James Morrison and oral tradition of Robert Good Voice. See, Leo Omani, "The Dakota Diaspora from Minnesota into Canada After 1862: Dispelling North American Colonial History in the Movement to Revive the Oral Dakota History, Language, and Culture of the Tiyospayes that Belong to Bdewakahton-

wan, Sisitonwan, Wahpetonwan, and Wahpekute," a paper delivered at the "Remembering, Retracing & Retelling: The Diaspora of the Dakota People from Minnesota into Canada and the Dakotas after 1862" Conference, Southwest Minnesota State University, Marshall, Minnesota, April 2001; and, J. Morrison, *Dakota/Lakota Joint Treaty Adhesion Project, Phase Two: Historical Land Use and Occupancy and Dakota/Lakota Crown Relations*, Legal Historical Research, Ancaster, Ontario, 2000.

3. For example, the Iowa, Oto, and Ho-Chunk all made their homes in Minnesota at various points.

4. Eldon Johnson, *The Prehistoric Peoples of Minnesota* (St. Paul: Minnesota Historical Society Press, 1988), 1.

5. For Northeastern origination, see Royal B. Hassrick, *The Sioux* (Norman: University of Oklahoma, 1964), 189. For East Coast originations, see Albert E. Jenks, "The Wild Rice Gatherers of the Upper Lakes: A Study in American Primitive Economics," *Nineteenth Annual Report of the Bureau of American Ethnology, 1897-98*, 19:2, 1043. For his information Jenks cites "Horatio Hale, The Tutelo Tribe and Language, Proc. *Am. Philos. Soc.*, vol. XXI, 1883-84; see also James Mooney, Siouan Tribes of the East, bulletin of the Bureau of Ethnology, 1894, and Horatio Hale, Indian Migrations, *Am. Antiquarian*, January and April, 1883."

6. See *Article 13* of the "United Nations Declaration on the Rights of Indigenous Peoples" which may be found at the Web site http://www.un.org/esa/socdev/unpfii/index.html (accessed September 13, 2007).

7. See Guy Gibbon, *The Sioux: The Dakota and Lakota Nations* (Malden, MA: Blackwell Publishers, 2003). I gave this work special attention because of its recent date of publication, demonstrating that recent decades of Indigenous Peoples challenging the colonialist presumptions and methods of anthropology have had little effect on old-school practitioners of the discipline. Instead, colonialist researchers still conduct research, as well as write and publish research that continues the academic tradition of dehumanizing, objectifying, and delegitimizing Indigenous presence in our lands.

8. See Eldon Johnson, *The Prehistoric Peoples of Minnesota* (St. Paul: Minnesota Historical Society Press, 1988), 28. Johnson merely reported the previous usage of such names as "Laurel," "Blackduck," "Kathio," "Malmo," and "Howard Lake" and would likely disagree with the characterization of this as a colonialist practice.

I should note that Dakota people do not deem all archeologists in Minnesota disrespectful and colonialist. Janet Spector, for example, conducted and documented her experiences with a nineteenth-century Dakota site, that of Mazomani's village along the Minnesota River. In addition to being ethically grounded and respectful of Dakota knowledge, many academics consider her research to be better informed, more accurate, and of a higher quality than other archeological works. See Janet D. Spector, *What This Awl Means: Feminist Archeology at a Wahpeton Dakota Village* (St. Paul: Minnesota Historical Society Press, 1993).

9. Roy Meyer discusses these early meetings in the first chapter of his book, *History of the Santee Sioux: United States Indian Policy on Trial* (Lincoln: University of Nebraska Press, 1967, 1993).

10. Gary Anderson, *Kinsmen of Another Kind: Dakota-White Relations in the Upper Mississippi Valley, 1650–1862* (St. Paul: Minnesota Historical Society Press, 1997), 19.

11. For example, William Folwell cites wars with the Iroquois as the reason for their forced migration as late as the mid-seventeenth century. See William Folwell, *A History of Minnesota, Volume I* (St. Paul: Minnesota Historical Society Press, 1956), 80. The Mille Lacs Band of Ojibwe Web site, for example, states, "Thousands of years ago, the Ojibwe were among several Indian tribes who lived on the Atlantic coast of North America. Then, about 500 years ago, many of these tribes began to migrate west as the eastern seaboard became colonized by the European settlers. Among them were the ancestors of the Mille Lacs Band of Ojibwe," see http://www.millelacsojibwe.org/culture.asp (accessed September 19, 2007).

12. See William W. Warren, *History of the Ojibway People* (St. Paul: Minnesota Historical Society Press, 1984), 76–81.

13. Edward Benton Banai, *The Mishoomis Book* (Hayward, WI: Indian Country Press, 1979), 94–102.

14. Father Hennepin lived from 1626 to 1705 and was sent on an exploratory mission by France in 1675. He was taken captive in 1680 by a war party of Dakota on the Mississippi. He spent three months as a Dakota prisoner before Sieur du Luth negotiated his release. For information about the locations of Dakota towns, see Newton H. Winchell, *The Aborigines of Minnesota* (St. Paul: The Pioneer Company, 1911), 73. It should be noted that the location of the Sisitunwans is a guess based

on a reference in Hennepin's report regarding the "Chongaskobe" that Winchell assumed to be them. Local accounts offer similar explanation. See, for example, Arthur P. Rose, *An Illustrated History of Yellow Medicine County* (Marshall, MN: Northern History Publishing Co., 1914), 19.

15. Winchell, *The Aborigines of Minnesota*, 64–65. Other archaeologists today might disagree with this analysis. However, a reading of the anthropological reports produced throughout the twentieth century about Minnesota's Indigenous inhabitants demonstrates the tremendous variety of what I would consider wildly contrasting opinions among "experts" regarding our origins. While feigning to deal in the realm of "truth" and "facts," it is clear that their rules for analysis are quite arbitrary and they would be comical if they did not negatively affect Indigenous Peoples. For example, when discussing evidence that suggests human populations in the Glacial epochs, Winchell notes the dismissal of evidence by some experts: "While probably most American geologists and archaeologists fully accept the foregoing as demonstrating the Glacial age of man in America, a few still remain skeptical, and with superfluous caution, or with carping criticism, call attention to defects in the evidence, and are inclined to explain all these instances by some accidental circumstances that may have caused intrusion of the specimens into the drift since the deposition of the same. Others attribute the reports to faulty observation and mistaken interpretation," 20. Scott Anfinson demonstrates that archaeologists still employ such practices nearly a century later stating, "Many of the dates from the Prairie Lake Region are either inaccurate (six deviate substantially from expectations and four others are less than 200 years old) or they have poor cultural associations." See, Scott F. Anfinson, *Southwestern Minnesota Archaeology: 12,000 Years in the Prairie Lake Region* (St. Paul: Minnesota Historical Society Press, 1997), 5. It seems to be a regular anthropological practice to simply dismiss whatever evidence (amassed according to their own methods and standards) does not support their reigning theory about the past. It thus makes it impossible to cite any anthropological work with a high degree of confidence.

16. Samuel Pond, *The Dakota or Sioux in Minnesota as They Were in 1834* (St. Paul: Minnesota Historical Society Press, 1986), 174. Carl Waldman asserts something similar in *Atlas of the North American Indian* (New York: Facts on File, 1985), 154.

17. See for instance Gary Anderson's *Kinsmen of Another Kind*.

18. Roy Meyer, *History of the Santee Sioux: United States Indian Policy on Trial* (Lincoln: University of Nebraska Press, 1967, 1993), 13.

19. William Warren, *History of the Ojibway People*, 61.

20. See, for example, the account of a descendant of a former chief from Mille Lacs, Warren, *History of the Ojibway People*, 157–58.

21. Warren, *History of the Ojibway People*, 161.

22. Ibid., 230–34.

23. See http://www.millelacsojibwe.org/ojibhistory.asp (accessed September 19, 2007).

24. William Watts Folwell, *A History of Minnesota, Volume I*, 148n42.

25. Ward Churchill discusses this in the context of international law. See Ward Churchill, *Perversions of Justice: Indigenous Peoples and AngloAmerican Law* (San Francisco: City Lights, 2003), 56.

26. Vine Deloria Jr., *Custer Died for Your Sins: An Indian Manifesto* (Norman: University of Oklahoma Press, 1988), 28. Originally published: New York: Macmillan, 1969. After 1969, Vine Deloria Jr. and Clifford Lytle acknowledged that over 600 treaties and agreements were made with Indigenous Peoples in the United States, stating, "Not only were these treaties designed, as was the first treaty, to ensure peaceful relations with the Indians but, even more important, they were also a means of securing an orderly transfer of landownership from the tribes to the United States." See Vine Deloria Jr. and Clifford Lytle, *American Indians, American Justice* (Austin: University of Texas Press, 1983), 3–4.

27. Meyer, *History of the Santee Sioux*, 26.

28. See "Endnotes" for the *Treaty with the Sioux Nation of Indians—1805*, compiled by Howard J. Vogel, Professor of Law, Hamline University School of Law. hvogel@hamline.edu.

29. Meyer, *History of the Santee Sioux*, 25–32.

30. For a discussion regarding the Catholic theological basis for acquiring Indigenous lands, see Vine Deloria Jr. and Clifford Lytle, *American Indians, American Justice*, 2–6.

31. Meyer, *History of the Santee Sioux*, 87.

32. Folwell, *A History of Minnesota*, 281, 284.

33. Meyer, *History of the Santee Sioux*, 79, 83.

34. Folwell, *A History of Minnesota*, 282.

35. An indication of the arbitrary and fraudulent nature of the

amounts paid to the traders is exemplified in the initial adjustment the traders made to scale down their claims in accordance with the treaties. In the case of the Treaty of Traverse des Sioux, for example, claims were reduced from $431,735.78 to $210,000. Sibley's claim alone was arbitrarily reduced from $144,984.40 to $66,459.00. See Folwell, *A History of Minnesota*, 283n37 through 303. In addition, Gary Anderson reports that Sibley's fur trade company alone took $105,618.54 that was divided among four White men: Sibley, Dousman, McLeod, and Ramsay Crooks, Anderson, *Kinsmen of Another Kind*, 197.

36. Folwell notes that the area has never been accurately computed, but cites other writers. Thomas Hughes computed "over 19,000,000 acres in Minnesota, nearly 3,000,000 acres in Iowa, and over 1,750,000 acres in South Dakota making in all nearly 24,000,000 acres of the choicest land on the globe," and the celebratory commissioner's report that stated that an area of 35,000,000 acres had been acquired. See Folwell, *A History of Minnesota*, 287.

37. Meyer, *History of the Santee Sioux*, 80–84.

38. Folwell, *A History of Minnesota*, 281. Folwell also notes that Ramsey helped negotiate a treaty with the Anishinabe at Pembina for the cession of some five million acres in the Red River Valley under similar terms with 5 percent interest payments for twenty years with the principal amount reverting back to the government at the end of that period. However, that treaty was not ratified by the Senate, 288, 291. Gary Anderson also comments that the money that was supposed to be held in trust was never put in the Treasury and Congress had to appropriate the interest each year, see Gary Clayton Anderson, *Kinsmen of Another Kind*, 186.

39. Anderson, *Kinsmen of Another Kind*, 197.

40. Meyer, *History of the Santee Sioux*, "Appendix: Treaty of Traverse des Sioux," 424–27.

41. Folwell, *A History of Minnesota*, 292.

42. Ibid., 297–99.

43. Anderson, *Kinsmen of Another Kind*, 196.

44. See "United Nations Convention on the Prevention and Punishment of the Crime of Genocide," http://www.ohchr.org/english/law/genocide.htm (accessed October 10, 2007).

45. Message of Governor Ramsey to the Legislature of Minnesota,

Delivered September 9, 1862 (St. Paul: WM. R. Marshall, State Printer, 1862), 12.

46. Meyer, *History of the Santee Sioux*, 126.

47. *The Guinness Book of Records* (New York: Bantam Books, 1993). Michael Yellow Bird cited this source in his article "Cowboys and Indians: Toys of Genocide, Icons of American Colonialism," *Wicazo Sa Review*, vol. 19, no. 2 (Fall 2004): 37. In addition, the History Channel recently debuted a program entitled "Wild West Tech: The Biggest Machines in the West" that detailed and celebrated the technological accomplishment embodied in the Mankato hangings. See http://store.aetv.com/html/product/index.jhtml?id=74170 (accessed October 11, 2007).

48. Folwell, *A History of Minnesota, Volume II*, 447–50.

49. See "Decolonizing the 1862 Death Marches," in Waziyatawin Angela Wilson, ed., *In the Footsteps of Our Ancestors: The Dakota Commemorative Marches of the 21st Century* (St. Paul: Living Justice Press, 2006).

50. Corinne L. Monjeau-Marz, *The Dakota Indian Internment at Fort Snelling, 1862-1864.* (St. Paul: Prairie Smoke Press, 2005), 54.

51. Ibid., 39.

52. Monjeau-Marz documents several of these examples in addition to the young women with their slit throats, such as the "squaw" reported killed during soldier's target shooting, later explained to be subjected to "infamous outrage." For further examples, see chapter 3, *The Dakota Indian Internment at Fort Snelling*.

53. Monjeau-Marz, *The Dakota Indian Internment at Fort Snelling*, 59.

54. Ibid., 60.

55. Ibid., 72.

56. Meyer, *History of the Santee Sioux*, 134.

57. Ibid., 135n3.

58. Raphael Lemkin who coined the term *genocide*, however, firmly believed that ethnocide was a form of genocide. "His definition included attacks on political and social institutions, culture, language, national feelings, religion, and the economic existence of the group." See, David Stannard, *American Holocaust: The Conquest of the New World* (New York: Oxford, 1992), quoting Frank Chalk and Kurt Jonassohn, 279.

59. Instances of boarding school abuses are being disclosed and documented every day. While corporal punishments included such acts as washing out children's mouths with lye for speaking Indigenous languages, forcing children to kneel for hours, whippings, beatings, strappings, other instances of abuse include rape and terrorism. These are documented in works such as Howard Adams, *Education for Extinction: American Indians and the Boarding School Experience* (Lawrence: University of Kansas Press, 1997), Ward Churchill, *Kill the Indian, Save the Man: The Genocidal Impact of American Indian Residential Schools* (San Francisco: City Lights Books, 2004), and Andrea Smith, *Conquest: Sexual Violence and the American Indian Genocide* (Cambridge: South End Press, 2005).

60. Smith, *Conquest*, 37.

61. David Stannard, *American Holocaust: The Conquest of the New World* (New York: Oxford, 1992), 120.

62. Ibid., 124.

63. Russell Thornton, *American Indian Holocaust and Survival: A Population History Since 1492* (Norman: University of Oklahoma Press, 1987), 50.

64. Stannard, *American Holocaust*, 125.

65. Meyer, *History of the Santee Sioux*, 140.

66. This is quoted in Meyer, *History of the Santee Sioux*, 146, though the quote is originally cited in Stephen Riggs, *Mary and I: Forty Years with the Sioux* (Boston: Congregational Sunday-School and Publishing Society, 1880), 224.

67. Thornton, *American Indian Holocaust and Survival*, 53–54. In this section Thornton also cites the work of scholar Sherburne Cook, "Demographic Consequences of European Contact with Primitive Peoples," *Annals of the American Academy of Political and Social Science*, 237, 1945: 107–11.

68. Andrea Smith provides an excellent discussion of sterilization in the larger context of attacks on Indigenous women's reproduction in her chapter "Better Dead than Pregnant," *Conquest: Sexual Violence and American Indian Genocide*, 80–88. See also Bruce Johansen, "Reprise/Forced Sterilizations: Native Americans and the Last Gasp of Eugenics," *Native Americas* 15 (Winter 1998): 44–47. Russell Means uses the overall sterilization rate of 42 percent for all women of childbearing

age. See Marvin J. Wolf, *Where White Men Fear to Tread: The Autobiography of Russell Means* (New York: St. Martin's Press, 1995), 375.

69. Smith, *Conquest*, 41.

70. See Curt Brown, "After Many Years, We Are Home," *Star Tribune*, Sunday, October 14, 2007, A1.

71. See Census 2000 PHC - -18. "American Indian and Alaska Native Tribes in Minnesota: 2000. Table 38—American Indians and Alaska Natives Alone and Alone or in Combination Population by Tribe for Minnesota: 2000." This information includes the 1,801 individuals self-identified as "Sioux" who might be Lakota or Nakota rather than Dakota. If those individuals are not factored in, the population of Dakota people would be 3,506. See also Northwest Area Foundation's "Indicators" Web site: http://www.indicators.nwaf.org/ (accessed December 19, 2007).

72. See Census 2000, "Table 1: American Indian and Alaska Native Population by Selected Tribal Grouping 2000" at www.census.gov/prod/2006pubs/censr-28.pdf (accessed December 19, 2007).

TWO

A Call for Truth Telling

*It is a consistent practice among progressives to
bemoan the genocide of Native peoples, but in the
interest of political expediency, implicitly sanction
it by refusing to question the legitimacy of the
settler nation responsible for this genocide.*

— ANDREA SMITH, *CONQUEST*

To many Minnesotans truth telling may seem an unnecessary
educational goal because there is no awareness of a denial of
truth. In this way, we could argue that contemporary citizens of
the state are residing in a kind of ideological matrix. The need
for truth telling espoused here assumes that what has passed for
the truth may not be truthful after all. It assumes that the educational system has not engaged our history in a satisfactory way
and that most Minnesotans still operate in the realm of myth
making. This means that many well-intentioned people, who
ordinarily would be horrified at the notion of being complicit
in the cover-up of genocide and the ongoing denial of justice for
Indigenous Peoples, have done just that. They have maintained
ignorance about this history while continuing to enjoy their
lives, unchallenged, in Dakota homeland at Dakota expense.

For those of us who believe in the transformative potential
of education, our hope derives from the expectation that once
people understand the truth, they will be compelled to act more
justly. Indeed, it has been my experience that the thought of
harming others disturbs most morally conscious individuals.
They are consequently upset when they learn the circumstances
regarding the invasion, conquest, and ethnic cleansing of Dakota

people from our homeland. Furthermore, once they reflect on the personal implications of harms perpetrated so their families could build futures in Dakota homeland, they also feel compelled to commit to some kind of corrective action. Most, however, have no idea how to conceptualize or implement such a monumental project for justice that would rectify historical harms. So, they simply continue with their lives, confining the awareness of ongoing injustices to the recesses of their minds.

When others learn about these historical harms, they are not moved. Fortunately, this group is generally in the minority. It includes the individuals who operate according to a bullying mentality ("We are the conquerors, so Indians just have to accept what happened," "Might makes right," "He who has the biggest or most weapons wins"). It also includes those who believe in the absolute superiority of White people and ways of being (and therefore the inferiority of all others, especially the "savage," "primitive Indians"). Still others in this minority group are so deeply invested in the myths and icons they have created, they will continue to defend them at all costs (those whose jobs or reputations depend on their preservation, for example).

In general, even these individuals do not dispute the facts surrounding the history relayed in the previous chapter because the amount of evidence is clear and compelling. Further, they do not disagree with the sources because many of them can be traced to White sources that they value and consider valid. For example, they do not attempt to deny Ramsey's declaration of extermination or forced removal or they do not attempt to disprove that the state offered bounties on Dakota scalps. They recognize that it would be entirely irrational and illogical to do so. Rather, they would disagree with the terminology and interpretive framework. They might dispute that what occurred in Minnesota constitutes genocide, for instance, charging faulty criteria perhaps. To maintain such a position, they have to disregard internationally agreed upon criteria concerning what constitutes genocide, in favor of some individually created definition developed spontaneously to attempt to refute the Dakota example. Or, they might insist on such a narrow perspective of history that the fault for Dakota ethnic cleansing rests squarely on the shoulders of Dakota people. Usually this is achieved by beginning the analysis with a discussion of Dakota violence against "innocent White settlers" in August 1862, thereby characterizing White violence as a mere response to unprompted Dakota attacks. To do this, they have to deny or ignore the long history of White violence that began when Whites first invaded Dakota homeland.

Sesquicentennial Discussion

Individuals have staked out these various positions in the public dialogue surrounding the Minnesota sesquicentennial that began appearing in the *Star Tribune* in fall 2007. In her column, Lori Sturdevant called for truth telling regarding Minnesota's early history, especially surrounding the "conflict resolution method of 1862" that she believes should never be repeated.[1] While various Dakota people and White supporters wrote letters in agreement with the notion that truth telling, no matter how painful, must be a part of the state agenda, others persisted with the myth making that has characterized elementary and secondary school curriculum about "Indians" since the 1860s.

For example, Patrick Hill, a resident of St. Paul and someone who has published on the Civil War in *Minnesota History* and *Ramsey County History* magazines, argued that justice was carried out in Mankato "Only if you believe a mere 38 individuals were responsible for the deaths of some 600 innocents and 100 defenders who sought to restore order."[2] His perversion of reality turns the usurpers into innocents and invaders into defenders of Indigenous land—that is an outright fabrication of the historical record. It is also a prime example of the colonizer's logic. However, what is most disturbing about Hill's openly racist and colonialist comment is that implicit in his argument is the notion

that Minnesotans did not go far enough in their policies of extermination and forced removal. Perhaps White Minnesotans
should have hanged all the Dakota warriors tried in 1862 and
perhaps they should have exterminated all the Dakota women
and children. That was certainly the ideology prevalent in the
1860s and Hill demonstrates it is alive and well in the minds of at
least some twenty-first-century Minnesota residents. However,
I would like to think that most Minnesotans today have moved
beyond that nineteenth-century genocidal mind-set.

Unfortunately, even though the research of professional historians has challenged the predominant narrative of "savage,
hostile, Sioux Indians rising up against unsuspecting and innocent White settlers" at least since the 1970s, that narrative largely
persists in the public history forums evident throughout the
state. The vast majority of public monuments surrounding 1862
and its aftermath have literally etched that narrative in stone,
especially those existing throughout southwestern Minnesota in
the towns affected most directly by the 1862 war. Other historic
sites and monuments, even those overseen by historical institutions, still actively suppress the story of genocide and ethnic
cleansing in Minnesota.

The Minnesota Historical Society continues to resist using
appropriate and accurate terminology such as "genocide," "ethnic cleansing," and "concentration camp," preferring instead more
benign terms that diminish the horror of Minnesota history.
This is not a reflection of ignorance, since the Minnesota Historical Society houses a lot of the evidence within their archives.
Instead, it is a reflection of ongoing racism and colonialism. As
an institution founded by the architect of Minnesota's genocidal
policies, Alexander Ramsey, the Minnesota Historical Society
has a definite legacy to uphold.

Another position in this debate is one in which the history is
addressed as though there exist multiple, equally valid perspectives. In this scenario, Dakota perspectives are just some among
many. This is the position taken by the Minnesota Sesquicenten-

nial Commission in the framework they have provided for Minnesota's 150th birthday party. Jane Leonard, the commission's
executive director, has stated on multiple occasions that she is
interested in including the Dakota perspective in sesquicentennial activities. With this in mind, she invited several Dakota
people (Neil McKay, Ramona Kitto Stately, and me) to present
on the history of Dakota genocide and ethnic cleansing before
the Sesquicentennial Commission in August 2007. No one
present disputed the evidence we presented, yet they also did
not engage the question posed to them at the end, "What does
recognition of genocide demand?" Recognizing that many Minnesotans have not encountered the truth of this history before,
we had hoped that an awareness of this story would persuade
them to rethink the notion of celebrating Minnesota statehood
in favor of a truth-telling agenda, since it is clear that Minnesotans achieved statehood at Dakota expense. This did not occur.
While no longer able to claim ignorance regarding this painful
history, the commissioners have chosen to ignore the important
question we posed to them and to reject truth telling as a major
sesquicentennial objective.

This poses a particular problem for Leonard who individually states she is committed to truth telling, but who still fails to
see the problems with her personal agenda. In the fall of 2007,
Leonard sought projects that could "wear a sesquicentennial
label and draw attention to the Dakota war story."[3] In another
article printed in 2008, she confessed a willingness to examine
Minnesota history, "warts and all." She also expressed a desire
to be "as inclusive as possible" in the telling, working from the
assumption that inclusivity is an appropriate response to Dakota
concerns.[4] Historian Annette Atkins agreed with Leonard, argu-
ing that while being attentive to additional narratives regarding
this past, "It would be a mistake to simply grieve our past . . . It
would be a mistake to cancel everything else and make this only
a time of confession."[5] On the surface, this seems to be a reasonable and fair argument. It implies a certain equity that appeals to

Americans, no special treatment for any one group, or privileging of one perspective over another. It is not until we examine this issue in a larger global context that the problems with this perspective become apparent.

If, for example, we use the example of the Holocaust as a frame of reference, simply because it provides the best-known and most widely accepted example of genocide by American audiences, the double standard employed in Minnesota becomes clear. When our educators teach about the Holocaust, they do not discuss the perpetration of genocide during World War II as part of the "Jewish perspective." They do not discuss the perpetration of genocide as just one perspective among many. They do not give validity to the Nazi rationale for perpetrating genocide. They do not celebrate the rise of the Third Reich that the Nazis achieved at Jewish expense. And, it would be considered unconscionable to teach about Nazi Germany without keeping the suffering of the victims of genocide at the forefront of the discussion. Instead, educators of the Holocaust take what might be termed a *moral perspective* on the Holocaust. That is, they teach from the assumption that the genocide against the Jews was a crime against humanity that cannot be rationalized from any valid perspective.

I would suggest that there is only one moral perspective on this aspect of Minnesota history. That is, that the genocide and ethnic cleansing perpetrated against Dakota people was a crime against humanity that cannot be rationalized from any valid perspective. Minnesotans achieved statehood at Dakota expense. If we take that position seriously, this critical "Dakota perspective" is not just one among many; it becomes the primary narrative around which we tell the rest of Minnesota history. It is unconscionable to teach about Minnesota history without keeping the suffering of the victims of genocide at the forefront of the discussion. Furthermore, until Dakota people achieve some kind of justice in regards to this shameful history, it is entirely inappropriate to celebrate what Minnesotans gained at Dakota expense. In this context, the issue does not represent a dichotomy between a Dakota perspective and a White perspective. There will always be Dakota people, or individuals with Dakota ancestry, who deny the harms perpetrated against Dakota people, and there will always be White people who acknowledge this history and how they have benefited from Dakota dispossession.

In the public dialogue surrounding the sesquicentennial, for example, John LaBatte (who appropriately takes the name *Wasicu Nazin* in Dakota or "Standing White Man" and claims Dakota ancestry) stated clearly in his 2007 letter to the editor, "Minnesota never committed genocide against the Indians." His statement thus serves to rationalize the mass hanging, bounties, and forced removals as a reasonable response to Dakota defense of homeland, as well as to eliminate their designation as crimes against humanity.[6]

On the other end, non-Dakota, critical thinking allies such as Louis Stanley Schoen, Paul Rivenburg, and Joe Tompkins submitted responses in defense of addressing historical harms perpetrated against the Dakota, or that demonstrated the absurdity of blaming the victims of genocide.[7] In addition, *Star Tribune* columnist Nick Coleman asked the poignant question in his December 23, 2007, commentary, "How do we talk like grown-ups about the war that made Minnesota at the same time we are celebrating the Eelpout Festival?" These examples demonstrate that this is not a Dakota versus White issue, but rather it is a twenty-first-century moral issue.

In addition, a point advanced by Dakota graduate student Erin Griffin around the sesquicentennial is that we cannot relegate truth telling to one Dakota corner of the sesquicentennial discussion table. Rather, just as Dakota people need to engage in telling our truths, colonizer society also needs to engage in their own truth telling. If the rest of Minnesota takes up truth telling and acknowledges how they have benefited from Dakota genocide and ethnic cleansing, remarkably similar narratives will emerge to the one advocated here. Furthermore, because Dakota people have been more likely to engage in truth telling surrounding this historical past, there is a much more pressing need for Whites to engage in their own truth telling.

That kind of truth telling differs from the numerous White accounts detailing how Dakota people killed White settlers (often depicted as brutal Indians savagely attacking innocent settlers). I must mention here that Dakota people do not deny that our ancestors killed White settlers in 1862. However, those of us who are more critically minded view those killings as part of Dakota defense of homeland. The stories of Dakota men killing White settlers remain the most prevalent in the historical landscape precisely because they feed a particular political project. Not only have these accounts been well documented and routinely recited in discussions surrounding the 1862 war, Minnesotans have firmly embedded them in the state's historical project. They do this because this narrative elicits images of Dakota savagery and brutality while denying the broader context in which those killings took place.

Bob Keller of New Hope exemplified the need of White settlers to put their personal narratives on par with Dakota loss of life during U.S. campaigns of genocide and ethnic cleansing. In a letter to the editor submitted to the *Star Tribune*, Keller relayed the account of the "murder" of his great-great-grandparents and their three-year-old daughter by "Indians" and asked at the end, "Oh, and if we're talking about reparations, where do I sign up for mine?"[8] Keller was concerned that in a previous letter to the editor, I had not provided the full context of genocide and ethnic cleansing by discussing all the White settlers killed by Dakota warriors in 1862, as if those killings would then effectively justify subsequent White actions. The broader context, however, is one in which Whites invaded Dakota homeland, frequently before any legal land cessions, with the expectation that they would dispossess Dakota people of our lands. In other words, everyone who came to Minnesota believed he or she had a superior right to Dakota land. There is nothing benign about that goal.

Moreover, anyone in the nineteenth century with the slightest understanding of Indigenous-White relations knew that Indigenous Peoples fought to protect their lands and ways of life. Thus, White settlers who moved into Indigenous lands did so knowing there might be risks from an "Indian" threat. Consequently, they pushed for the United States government and military to subjugate Indigenous populations by any means necessary, usually as quickly as possible. This, too, is not a benign expectation. Thus, in attempting to place the killing of his ancestors on par with Dakota victims, Keller attempts to uphold the righteousness of invasion, conquest, genocide, and ethnic cleansing. This is not a strong moral position, nor does it make sense given the broader historical view.[9]

Furthermore, in his half-hearted inquiry about reparations, Keller fails to recognize that his family already received compensation for the risk his ancestors took in living on the frontier. His family got the land. Keller is still occupying Dakota homeland while most Dakota people are not.

Dakota Responses to This Historical Legacy

Because of Minnesota's policies of genocide, ethnic cleansing, and colonization, the Dakota became a diasporic nation, with populations scattered throughout five states in the U.S. and two provinces in Canada. Since 1862 we have also remained a scarred people, never fully exerting our humanity for fear that settler society would further diminish us as a people. Social conditions in our communities are the litmus tests for our well-being and they reflect a people in pain. Our people suffer from high rates of family violence, sexual abuse, chemical dependency, diabetes, and suicide across the board. That is, I do not know of a single community in the United States or Canada that is not dealing with all of these issues. Most debilitating, however, is the notion that we are to blame for all of these conditions. For almost 150 years our people have lived daily with both guilt and fear, afraid to hope for a better future. Most of our people attempted to cope with the pain of our past by forgetting. Our people spoke many stories about 1862 in hushed tones or in secret so the dominant society would not know we still remembered these stories of injustices. Many other stories went untold, dying with the victims of *Wasicu* cruelty and greed, unknown to the future generations.

Nevertheless, amazing transformation occurs when we bring these stories to the light of day and we begin to dwell on them. We go through stages of disbelief, pain, and outrage, and while those feelings never seem to depart completely, they create a new feeling of empowerment. If we think deeply about the pain of our ancestors, we become more aware of our own pain and how our pain is connected to that of our ancestors. In addition, if we allow ourselves a little hope, we can imagine a time when we might be relieved of our suffering. But, because our current pain is connected to our ancestors' pain, we also start to realize that our suffering cannot be relieved unless contemporary injustices are addressed, until we are allowed to live as Dakota people once again. This, my relatives, is magic because it allows us to wake up from our colonial slumber. When we recognize the current state of colonization, we can begin to work toward a decolonized future.

The Power of Truth

For example, in 2002, a group of Dakota people decided to venture into that place of inconsolable grief, and none of us really knew what the outcome would be. We understood, however, that it was important for us to retrace the 150-mile route that our ancestors were forced to march in 1862, the march that marked the first phase of Dakota expulsion from our homeland. This was the first ever Dakota Commemorative March. What began as an effort to remember and honor our ancestors who suffered in 1862, primarily the women and children, eventually developed into a strengthening of our people through an empirical understanding of what extensive suffering does to an Indigenous nation.

As we walked, mile by mile, placing prayer stakes in the earth and calling out the names of our ancestors, we mourned the losses our people endured. We mourned for the loss of life taken in 1862, we mourned for the loss of our ability to grieve in the accustomed manner, and we mourned for the loss of our homeland and all the beings who once inhabited the land with us. Through our tears and our aching bodies, we contemplated the meaning of the forced removal of our ancestors and began to weigh the costs. As we observed what has replaced us in our homeland— the towns, streets, businesses, houses, and "development"—we allowed ourselves to compare the Dakota life that once was with what is in existence now. The comparison left us stunned.

In our ancestors' footsteps, we revealed the lies the colonizers used to indoctrinate our people about our own inferiority. Our beautiful *Minisota* landscape had become desecrated in the name of *Wasicu* progress and a hopelessly unsustainable way of life. With each step on the march, we were untwisting the perverted logic that characterizes colonial doctrine. We began to realize down to the core of our beings just how wrong it is to remove a nation of people from their homeland. As we reconnected with our homeland and the spirits of our ancestors, we understood the magnitude of the horror settler society perpetrated against us in the 1860s. We were discovering truth.

As the marchers struggled through sorrow and rage, I think many of us sensed that such crimes against humanity cannot be left unresolved. They demand our attention and our action. They demand our imaginations. Diane Wilson captured this intellectual transformation in her writing about the 2004 Commemorative March stating, "When I listened, I heard words that told me there was another way, one that had been trampled on, beat up, abused, but that still carried a strong message of hope and truth. It was like hearing a song I had almost forgotten, its melody familiar and strange all at once."

We can never completely alleviate our grief, but it is in this grieving space that we can use our grief as a conduit to a state of empowerment. That is, we will never stop grieving over the genocide perpetrated against our people by White Minnesotans. No people can ever heal completely from such a devastating wound. However, we can strengthen our people and pick up the struggle for liberation our ancestors initiated in the 1860s. We can honor their suffering and their memory by instituting a calculated and strategic effort toward reclamation of our homeland.

When I reflected on the march experiences, I wrote, "Acknowledging the humanity of our ancestors awakens us to our own humanity—as well as to the realization that we, too, are worthy of justice and freedom from oppression."[10] It is that sentiment that convinces me of the need for a broad-scale truth-telling and reparations agenda.

A Truth-Telling Forum

At the conclusion of the Truth and Reconciliation Commission in South Africa, Archbishop Desmond Tutu stated, "No one in South Africa could ever again be able to say, 'I didn't know,' and hope to be believed."[11] For decades, White South Africans and even many black South Africans denied the horrors perpetrated during apartheid, turning a blind eye toward the brutality, violence, dehumanization, and severe oppression that characterized the lives of the majority population living amongst them. Thus, exposing the truth of that history unmasked the racism and colonialism that allowed those relations to continue and it named them for what they were. As a result, they exposed the most virulent racists and colonialists who tried to continue to espouse ignorance and deny the history of oppression. Most eventually chose to reject that course of action and embrace the truth, no matter how painful, with the hope that they could create a more just society for everyone.

Clearly, Minnesotans as a whole are still in a phase of ignorance and denial. There is no thought given by most residents of the state as to how their occupation of Dakota homeland affected Dakota people of the past or how it still affects Dakota people of today. Though many might maintain a vague sense that Dakota people were treated unfairly or ripped off in some way, for most, even that injustice is considered a thing of the past. From that perspective, it is easy to understand why the attitude that "Indians need to stop whining about the past and just get over it" is still prevalent. How, after all, would Minnesotans have learned anything different? They certainly would not have learned a different perspective in the existing educational system. Unfortunately, Minnesota schools still typically deny or suppress the history of genocide, ethnic cleansing, concentration camp internment, and the ongoing colonization of Dakota people.

In many ways, this denial of truth is the crux of the problem that disallows any meaningful movement toward justice. For if settler society denies the injustices of the past and present, then the impetus to maintain the status quo is strong; there is no recognized need for change. It is only when injustices are recognized that a momentum for dramatic change can be achieved.

Few Minnesotans are aware of the ongoing oppression faced by Dakota people, nor do they understand our past oppression in what I would call a longer view of history. When the settlers invaded, they wreaked havoc on the Dakota way of life. There was no aspect of our ways of being that did not come under aggressive attack. Missionaries, government agents, traders, and *Wasicu* settlers all worked together to simultaneously assault and attempt to destroy all that made us Dakota people. In addition to attacking the traditional subsistence patterns that allowed us to live sustainably for thousands of years, the foreigners attacked our economy, our spirituality, our language, our dress, our hair, our foods, our educational system, and the most essential elements of being Dakota, our bodies and our lands. This kind of wholesale assault made living peacefully impossible.

No nation could survive these kinds of attacks and the *Wasicus* certainly expected that the Dakota would be no exception.

When our people finally declared war on the United-States government in 1862, we did so after they pushed us to the absolute brink. This, too, was no miscalculation. If the Dakota took up weapons against the U.S. government and its citizens, then Americans could justify, with citizen support, a full-scale military assault. Further, the government could then rationalize policies of extermination and a total land grab, all with the support and sanctioning of Minnesota residents specifically, and U.S. citizens more broadly. In the end, our war would serve U.S. purposes because the United States could use our violence to convince even more liberal-minded Americans about our savagery. Our capacity and ability to be Indigenous in our homeland consequently ended.

If we then fast-forward to the twenty-first century and examine what has changed, we see that in spite of casinos, it is very little. As mentioned previously, the vast majority of Dakota people still live in exile, while those who reside here maintain tiny land bases. Even when our existing communities attempt to buy back the land settler society stole from us, private landowners, as well as county, state, and federal authorities, frequently hinder or prevent those land purchases. Then, if we are lucky and persistent enough to work our way through the colonialist land tenure system and bureaucratic red tape, Minnesota residents continue to attack Dakota people for not paying various taxes on our stolen land.[12] The irony and injustice of that seems to escape them. These problems exist for all the Dakota communities in Minnesota, including those with plenty of money to attempt land buyback. Meanwhile, we watch as other Minnesotans enjoy their occupation of Dakota homeland unfettered by even the slightest encumbrance of guilt or critical self-reflection.

Furthermore, we live in a society that has largely renamed and remade the landscape. At one time Dakota people had names for everything in the state and it was our worldview that was reflected back to us in the landscape. Now that is not the case. While vestiges of our place names remain in Anglicized versions—places like Chaska, Winona, Wayzata, Owatonna, and even Minnesota—White Minnesotans erased most of our original presence from the landscape. They severely altered the natural environment through the elimination of biodiversity, the draining of wetlands, the stripping of forests, the desertification of the prairies, the extraction of natural resources, unrelenting "development," and the continuous pollution of the waters, air, and land. Prior to European invasion, Indigenous Peoples occupied this land sustainably for thousands of years without this kind of wholesale and, in some instances, irreversible destruction. Since achieving statehood 150 years ago, Minnesotans have perpetrated unprecedented harm upon Dakota homeland on a magnitude that is almost incomprehensible.

From the perspective of our worldview, the devastation to our homeland is a mirror reflection of what has happened to our people. Because the fate of our people is intertwined with the fate of our homeland, we grieve when she is harmed. Since the United States government has achieved sovereignty over the land, the story of the land has been one long, uninterrupted tale of devastation.

Yet, for the most part, Dakota people have been powerless to prevent much of this devastation. Even amidst tremendous resistance, Dakota people at Prairie Island in the last half of the twentieth century, for example, were unable to prevent the development of Northern States Power Company's nuclear facility adjacent to their reservation, nor the dry cask storage of nuclear waste that came later. Indeed, that example provides a perfect insight into how government and corporations have worked against Indigenous Peoples, as it was the Bureau of Indian Affairs that negotiated with NSP for right of way through the Prairie Island reservation to the severe detriment of the Dakota population and the land.[13]

In the Minnesota River Valley, we currently face a similar threat by the proposed creation of Big Stone II, a coal-fired power plant at the headwaters of the Minnesota River, just across the border in Big Stone City, South Dakota. In addition to draining public water sources and emitting millions of tons of CO_2 every year, Big Stone II would also emit mercury that would end up in the Minnesota River, as its older brother Big Stone I has already done for forty years. The existing Dakota communities of Upper and Lower Sioux are downwind, downgrade, and downstream from that toxin-producing mess. Furthermore, because of its close proximity to Big Stone I and proposed Big Stone II, the Lake Traverse reservation is also facing threats to their people, lands, water, and air. The Minnesota River is now so toxic that American Rivers, a national environmental organization based in Washington, DC, recently named it to the 2008 Top Ten List of America's most endangered rivers. While we are mobilizing with White allies to prevent the development of Big Stone II, we can only hope that Minnesota and South Dakota residents will recognize that this environmental devastation is harmful to all of us.[14]

For example, the Twin Cities metropolitan area is now facing the effects of industrial pollutants such as 3M's groundwater contamination from decades of dumping perfluorochemicals into the landfills that then flowed into groundwater and the Mississippi River. Moreover, as we experience the effects of global warming, we know no one will be immune from the effects of environmental polluting.

In all areas, including the regulation of environmental standards, Dakota people are subject to the imposition of the colonizers' systems and institutions within our homeland. These systems and institutions disallow us from being Dakota every day of our lives. For example, if we attempted to enforce environmental standards according to our worldview and ethic, we would risk lawsuits, incarceration, or death. Thus, our homeland has been subject to the colonizers' environmental ethic.

Our children are subject to the colonizers' educational system. If we decided to keep our children home to raise them according to our traditional educational expectations, we would risk state intervention and the theft of our children.

If we wanted to engage in a subsistence lifestyle, which would require going off reservation because of our exceptionally small land bases today, we would risk citation and arrest for trespassing, as well as hunting, fishing, and land-use violations. Subsistence living is also currently limited by the environmental degradation caused by the culture of exploitation and consumption in the dominant society. Yet, if in an effort to recover subsistence ways, we challenge too strenuously the corporations, business owners, farmers, and individuals who have desecrated our homeland, we would face incarceration.

Similarly, if we wanted to access our sacred sites in our homeland or engage in ceremonies at specific locations, there too we would face citation or arrest for trespassing, as well as fines for fee or access violations. Perhaps we would even face charges of indecent exposure.

If we rejected colonizer criminal and social welfare institutions in favor of our traditional system of justice and social welfare by refusing to subject our people to county, state, or federal authorities, the police would likely surround our reservations and blockade all our access. Then they, and perhaps even the military, would infiltrate our communities and threaten us with incarceration or death.

If we attempted to reject the capitalist system and return to a traditional economic system, that would ensure almost instant conflict with the dominant society's institutions and systems. The U.S. government attempts to squash any system or activities they cannot regulate, using whatever force is necessary. For example, the U.S. would immediately deem unregulated and untaxed trade as illegal and would likely view it as a threat to national security.

In essence, it is virtually impossible to practice indigeneity or Dakota ways of being in our homeland today without bumping up against powerful and oppressive institutions and facing severe repercussions to our families, our communities, and ourselves.

Consequently, most of our people have learned not to regularly challenge these systems and institutions, or we are selective about which ones we challenge so as not to suffer all the negative repercussions at once. We have learned to get along in the colonizers' systems, and some of our people never allow themselves to think about how limited our lives have become, how controlled, how regulated by the state. Furthermore, the severe repression occurring because of this controlled, limited existence only compounds the trauma we still experience from historical harms.

In addition, we experience many minor assaults on a daily basis. For example, the frame of reference taken for granted by members of the dominant society almost never includes Dakota people. Thus, when we hear the word "we" in any dominant society context, Dakota people are almost never included—in fact, for the non-Dakota readers, this may be one of the first texts you have encountered in which the "we" in this book refers specifically to Dakota people, rather than to the dominant society.

When we hear about history, philosophy, spirituality, science, math, culture, music, it almost never refers to Dakota conceptions of history, philosophy, spirituality, science, math, culture, or music. When our conceptions are referenced, they are accompanied with qualifying adjectives that indicate our conceptions are not on the same level as the colonizers'.

In fact, the dominant society generally still considers inferior all aspects of our ways of being. Colonizing society reinforces these messages on a daily basis through the educational system, the popular media, and our work and recreational experiences. They continue to appropriate our images and traditions and mock us as sports mascots and in print advertising. The dominant society rarely assumes that we have anything of value to offer the world . . . except our resources. Though meager they may now be, colonizing society continues to threaten what remains of those resources. Moreover, they assume that we are not as intelligent, not as creative, not as competent, and not as hard working, as are those in settler society.

Like other oppressed Peoples in the United States, because we are darker skinned, individuals from the colonizing society are more likely to deny us access to rental apartments or housing, to provide us bank loans to purchase houses, to provide interviews and offer jobs, and to provide us equal pay or recognize us with promotions in competition with White colleagues. Law enforcement is more likely to profile and harass us, to administer harsher sentences for smaller crimes, and to ensure our people stay subjugated through incarceration. Educational systems are more likely to single us out as slower learners and to maintain low expectations for achievement. Business owners are more likely to watch us and follow us in stores when we are shopping, and to treat us rudely when we are patronizing their businesses. These are the unpleasant realities we experience when we are trying to fit in and when we are attempting to abide by colonial rules and regulations. Few from the colonizing society recognize the struggles faced daily by Dakota people as we attempt to negotiate a society that strips us of our humanity at every turn.

If after Minnesotans perpetrated the heinous crimes of genocide and ethnic cleansing, the assaults on Dakota people ceased and the colonizer population sought to restore justice for Dakota people and support our ways of being, our populations would likely have been able to recover. However, that is not what happened. After the assaults of the 1860s, the attacks simply took on different forms and they continue to the present day.

In addition, White Minnesotans have never attempted to undo the wrongs perpetrated so that Dakota people might recover the ways of life that sustained us as human beings, nor have Minnesotans made a concerted effort to ensure our access to our homeland. I would suggest the primary reason that this continues to occur is that they have not recognized the truth of our oppression. Instead, in addition to our ongoing oppression, settler society continues to deny our humanity through the lack of recognition of the genocide and ethnic cleansing perpetrated against us. When the colonizing society denies us acknowledgment, it alerts us to the reality that they still deem us an expendable population. We are still unworthy human beings. Thus, we simply add this denial to the long list of crimes perpetrated against us.

Denial of Genocide as a Crime

Denial of genocide is a crime. Many nations from the global community recognize the importance of acknowledging genocide. In parts of Europe, for example, it is a crime to deny the Holocaust. They consider Holocaust denial an egregious form of anti-Semitism. The justice system has consequently charged and imprisoned individuals for this offense. Historian David Irving was imprisoned for a year in Austria for denying the Holocaust while far-right, British National Party leader Nick Griffin has been routinely prosecuted for inciting racial hatred. In November 2007, Oxford University was under attack for providing a forum for Irving and Griffin to express their views.[15] This invoked in the United States the recent memory of the controversy that erupted in September 2007 at Columbia University when Iranian President Mahmoud Ahmadinejad was invited to speak despite his vehement and persistent denial of the Holocaust.

In another instance in January 2008, a judge sentenced a German lawyer, Sylvia Stolz, to three and half years in jail for denying the Holocaust. She has made a practice of defending Holocaust deniers, even ending one of her legal briefs with "Heil Hitler."[16] Yet, in Minnesota, citizens and the legal system do not criminalize the denial of genocide and ethnic cleansing. In fact, Minnesotans do just the opposite. Minnesotans typically celebrate the perpetrators of genocide. They also routinely attack those of us who speak the truth about this history, often ridiculing, marginalizing, or dismissing our desire to seek recognition and justice.

Wide-Scale Truth Telling

The antidote to this is wide-scale truth telling. As Dakota people, we must take up the task of telling the truths of the oppression in our historical and contemporary experiences. We must present those truths in a variety of forums until knowledge about the genocide, ethnic cleansing, and oppression becomes a part of the consciousness of all Minnesotans and it infiltrates public awareness. Only then will people at all levels of society, from children to corporate leaders and politicians, recognize a need for justice.

As Dakota people, we need advocates of truth telling within our communities who can initiate community discussions about the need to engage in truth-telling activities. I have already outlined a potential process for collecting evidence in the volume *For Indigenous Eyes Only: A Decolonization Handbook*, based on many of the strategies used by the Truth Commission into Genocide in Canada.[17] Briefly, the first stage involves engaging community, organizational, or group discussions to gauge the relevancy of and need for a truth-telling process. Then communities can work to develop a collective, critical consciousness regarding the ongoing injustices. If individuals and groups determine a need for truth telling, they can then implement strategies to collect testimonies and supporting data. Because this is a process that will take time and tremendous effort, no one person needs to undertake this project for the entire Dakota nation. In fact, as a nation, the more people who are involved with this project, the greater success we will achieve.

Individuals, for example, might decide to collect testimony or evidence specifically related to their own family or community. While we will eventually have to compile the evidence and testimonies in one or more places, we can all help to support such a project. Our tribal colleges and school classrooms can assist in collecting data and serving as repositories of information. The kind of evidence to collect will be testimonies about personal experiences, oral histories that reflect the experiences of our ancestors, and other primary and secondary sources that provide additional evidence of human injustices.

During this phase, our communities will need to institute aggressive healing measures to help process the grief that arises when we begin to disclose painful truths. As the Dakota Oyate is already in a period of rebirth in which traditional ceremonial life is becoming increasingly more central to the lives of our communities, these ceremonies will play a vital role in supporting our efforts. Yet, as we have discovered in other truth-telling venues, we have no traditional practices for recovering from genocide and ethnic cleansing. Because it was only when Euro-Americans implemented those policies in the nineteenth century that we first encountered those kinds of crimes against humanity, we have not created ways to adequately heal from them. Thus, as a nation of people, we must work with our spiritual leaders to find a way to heal spiritually from genocide.

The next step involves initiating a public educational campaign at the local, state, national, and international levels. We can facilitate this phase through the work of both Dakota people and our non-Dakota allies. Initially newspapers and other media outlets can support this project, just as they have in other truth commission projects in other parts of the world. White communities and organizations can offer resolutions of support for the truth-telling process; push for the recognition of genocide, ethnic cleansing, and ongoing colonization; and offer their support to the Dakota community as a matter of ethical responsibility. When substantial amounts of evidence are available, Dakota people will need to organize the evidence and incorporate it into a coherent narrative so that we can submit it to state, federal, and international bodies that can hear and address Dakota grievances. Educators can also use this body of evidence, or appropriate portions of it, as an important teaching tool for classrooms and other educational institutions and forums.

The educational campaign has already begun. This project

is part of it. However, Dakota individuals have been speaking out for decades regarding the injustices experienced by Dakota people. In my generation, individuals such as Chris Mato Nunpa, Gabrielle Tateyuskanskan, Dave Larsen, and Elizabeth Cook-Lynn have worked tirelessly to educate Americans about this darker side of American history and the treatment of Dakota people. Many individuals before them also kept alive the memories of suffering and the spirit of resistance within our families and communities. Even when there was no one to stand beside them, many of our people, fearlessly and courageously, have engaged in truth telling.

Our non-Dakota allies can also facilitate the truth-telling process by talking with their families, friends, and communities in support of this project. Allies can share this volume—pass it around or buy additional volumes to contribute to community forums. Allies can contact their local media outlets and encourage them to engage the truth-telling project. To achieve the kind of broad-scale truth telling that will be necessary to reach everyone, we have to tell, relentlessly, the story of genocide and ethnic cleansing. The difficulty of this should not be underestimated. It is emotionally and spiritually exhausting to dwell in such a difficult space. In addition, many non-Dakota people may become overwhelmed by the information and consequently believe they should not have to hear about it more than once. However, in order to move on to the next phase of action, we all have to contemplate deeply the implications of this history, understand the magnitude of the suffering for Dakota people, and then take action to achieve justice. This will not happen after the first time Whites contemplate these truths.

It is that deep understanding, however, that will provide the way out of the suffering for us all. That is when all of us will achieve a state of empowerment. It is extraordinarily important then, when Dakota people engage in truth telling, that our allies stand up to support us. It is very difficult to stand alone, and we do so when we have to because we cannot imagine doing anything else, but standing alone is wearisome. It is imperative for individuals to speak out in support of our efforts if they are in agreement with the Dakota struggle for justice. Silence suggests complicity with the status quo. To not speak out is to engage in the crime of genocide denial and to perpetrate another crime against humanity.

Truth telling has the potential to alleviate the burden that all of us carry—Dakota people who carry historical trauma and the pain of ongoing oppression and White Minnesotans who carry the burden of maintaining oppressive systems and institutions. The denial of humanity to Minnesota's Original People is a burden carried by all Minnesotans. Truth telling allows us to relieve those burdens and take the next step toward justice. It allows us to engage the question: What does recognition of genocide demand?

Notes

1. Lori Sturdevant, "A time when cultures met—and clashed," *Star Tribune*, October 28, 2007, http://www.startribune.com/opinion/commentary/11150686.html. Also see my response to the Sturdevant column, Waziyatawin Angela Wilson, "The Sesquicentennial 150 Years of Statehood: Time to Level," Sunday, December 2, 2007, OP1–2. These and many of the related articles are available through www.waziyatawin. blogspot.com.

2. Patrick Hill, "Patrick Hill: The rest of the settlement story," *Star Tribune*, December 6, 2007.

3. Sturdevant, "A time when cultures met—and clashed."

4. Kevin Duchschere, "State's birthday bash is on a tight budget," *Star Tribune*, January 1, 2008, A1 & A10.

5. Ibid., A10.

6. John LaBatte, "Letter of the day: Two different views of the Dakota Uprising," *Star Tribune*, December 19, 2007.

7. See "Louis Stanley Schoen: We must talk about race, despite the difficult emotions it stirs," *Star Tribune*, December 30, 2007; "Paul Rivenburg: Minnesota's 150th Cake and Reconciliation," *Star Tribune*,

December 9, 2007; and, "Joe Tompkins: 'Settlement story': genocide by another name," *Star Tribune*, December 10, 2007.

8. Bob Keller, letter to the editor, "First came an uprising," *Star Tribune*, Sunday, December 9, 2007.

9. For further discussion regarding White culpability, see Wilson, ed., *In the Footsteps of Our Ancestors*, 60–62.

10. Wilson, ed., *In the Footsteps of Our Ancestors*, 263.

11. Desmond Tutu, *No Future Without Forgiveness* (New York: Doubleday, 1999), 120.

12. It should be noted that Dakota individuals living off-reservation are required to pay the same taxes as any other citizen and that the only exemption for on-reservation Dakota people are state taxes and property taxes while federal taxes are still paid. And, our reservation lands are legally "owned" by the United States government and held in trust for us.

13. See Winona LaDuke's discussion of Prairie Island in *All Our Relations: Native Struggles for Land and Life* (Cambridge: South End Press, 1999), 106–108.

14. Clean-Up the River Environment (CURE) is working to oppose Big Stone II in defense of the Minnesota River Valley. For further information, visit their Web site at www.curemnriver.org/.

15. Mark Rice-Oxley, "In Britain, Free Speech for Far-Right?" *Christian Science Monitor*, November 27, 2007, http://www.csmonitor.com/2007/1127/p07s01-woeu.html (accessed January 5, 2008).

16. "Mannheim, Germany: Holocaust denier jailed," *The Week*, January 25, 2008.

17. Waziyatawin, "Relieving Our Suffering: Indigenous Decolonization and a United States Truth Commission," in Waziyatawin Angela Wilson and Michael Yellow Bird, eds., *For Indigenous Eyes Only: A Decolonization Handbook* (Santa Fe: School of American Research Press, 2005), 189–205.

THREE

Taking Down the Fort

> *A world divided into compartments, a motionless,*
> *Manicheistic world, a world of statues: the statue of*
> *the general who carried out the conquest, the statue*
> *of the engineer who built the bridge; a world which*
> *is sure of itself, which crushes with its stones the*
> *backs flayed by whips: this is the colonial world.*
>
> — FRANTZ FANON, *WRETCHED OF THE EARTH*

After the initial wave of explorers and traders came to *Minisota,* the next wave of invaders came more loudly. This group of U.S. Army soldiers built Fort St. Anthony in 1819 with the intention of establishing U.S. dominance in the region and preparing the way for *Wasicu* settlement. In 1825, it was renamed Fort Snelling after one of the commanding officers, Colonel Josiah Snelling. This imposing structure became *Minisota's* first monumental icon of American imperialism. Built of stone and mortar, Americans intended for this structure to last, a seemingly permanent and gigantic reminder that Dakota homeland was in the predatory sights of the U.S. government. The influx of *Wasicu* settlers, who came to displace the Dakota population so that they could obtain some of the richest farmland in the country, served as the precursors of U.S. hegemony. By the mid-nineteenth century, this was a story that had played out hundreds of times among Indigenous populations in various regions of what would eventually become the United States we know today. The outcome for most Indigenous Peoples was largely the same: extermination, ethnic cleansing, dispossession, and cultural eradication. It was the same for the Dakota.

Fort Snelling still stands as this moniker of imperialism. In spite of its purpose and history, because it has marked the landscape for so long, many of us have come to accept it as a permanent fixture. We have normalized the presence of the site in our lives. This is true even for many Dakota people who cannot conceive of a landscape without the fort. Yet, mortar and stone crumbles. Even if we did nothing, the fort would fall. In fact, it has only been through the systematic and faithful efforts of White Minnesotans that the fort continues to be resuscitated. Human activities, fires, gravity, and Minnesota weather have jeopardized the fort on more than one occasion and Minnesotans have had to reinvest consciously in their icon of imperialism in order to save it.

For example, as the Minnesota Historical Society's Web site on Fort Snelling explains, "For most of this century [20th century], little remained of the frontier fort built in the early 1820s."[1] It was not until the 1950s when demolition was imminent that efforts to save Fort Snelling achieved considerable success. After a proposed interstate loop located at the site of the Round Tower threatened the fort, state citizens helped to launch a massive campaign to declare Fort Snelling a national historic landmark (1960) and restore it to its 1820s condition.[2] Thus, the fort that people visit today is not the original Fort Snelling; it is a manufactured replica.

While I do not know of any Dakota people who like Fort Snelling and what it represents, for the most part, as colonized people we have come to accept it as part of the unchangeable reality of colonization. A series of events surrounding the fort in the last several years, however, has caused many of us to engage in critical reflection about the site.

The Plans to Re-Fortify the Fort

The most recent event is the controversy that surrounds the Minnesota Historical Society's plans to use millions of dollars of Minnesota taxpayers' money to fund a major fort renovation. I first learned of the renovation plans for the fort in 2004 through the ideas circulating about an Ojibwe and Dakota language center at Historic Fort Snelling in the circuit of academic conferences in Indigenous Studies. Brenda Child (an Anishinabe historian and associate professor of American Studies at the University of Minnesota and executive board member for the Minnesota Historical Society) proposed the original plans for the center. Child and a few of her students then elaborated on these plans during a formal session at the American Society for Ethnohistory Conference in Santa Fe in November 2005. In a presentation entitled "Reclaiming Fort Snelling," they articulated a plan for a Dakota/Ojibwe language and culture institute that the Minnesota Historical Society would create in the renovated soldier's barracks of the historic fort.

While I was unable to attend the conference in Santa Fe because of my commitment to attend our Commemorative March ceremonies at Lower Sioux near that time, I was concerned about any plans that would connect Dakota cultural initiatives with an institution of colonialism. Also disconcerting was the inclusion of Ojibwe history and culture at a site with such deep meaning to Dakota people. As the Ojibwe have no claim to the Mendota area, there was really no reason for their inclusion in any discussion pertaining to it. Indeed, Indigenous Peoples generally respect another People's claim to a site and it was disturbing that Child was not assuming Dakota primacy in the plans she was creating. I became more concerned when Ho-Chunk scholar Amy Lonetree, who attended this session at the Ethnohistory Conference, described how Child used images of the Commemorative March to endorse her plan. By appropriating the Commemorative March images, Child and her students were suggesting that this proposed Fort Snelling project extended the aims of our attempts to remember and honor our ancestors imprisoned in the concentration camp at Fort Snelling during the winter of 1862–1863. We were deeply committed to engaging a truth-telling agenda for our Commemorative Marches; however, the proposed Fort Snelling project was interested in just the opposite.

When the University of Minnesota's American Indian Studies Department belatedly called a community meeting to discuss the project in February 2006, it was clear there was deep concern over the issue amidst the Dakota community. We estimate that between 120 and 140 people attended the public meeting, most of them Dakota. We heard introductions from Pat Albers, then chair of American Indian Studies at the U of M, and from Brenda Child. It was apparent right from the beginning that neither of these individuals understood how deeply this project was embedded in colonialist ideology.

Child began the February meeting by linking the renovation of Fort Snelling to the Minnesota Historical Society's celebration of Minnesota statehood. In this context, the language institute would serve a revitalizing function for Dakota and Ojibwe languages. However, it would also simultaneously reify the overarching master narrative that celebrates White settlement in Minnesota at the expense of Dakota claim to our lands. This mixed message was confirmed in the proposed plan, "Bdote: Where the Rivers Meet," circulated by Child. The proposal promoted the benefits of a language institute saying, "With Bdote historically being an area of interaction, diplomacy and communication among Minnesota's Indigenous nations and other nations, the Center for Dakota Iapi and Ojibwemowin can honor that past as becoming a place where the Dakota and Ojibwe nations once again interact and communicate with each other and with the general public as well."[3] In emphasizing communication and interaction, this proposal glosses over the genocidal role the fort played in 1862–63 and reaffirms the benign narrative also espoused by literature produced at Historic Fort Snelling.

For example, the Fort Snelling literature makes no mention of the fort as an outpost of American imperialism that served

as a harbinger of the establishment of American military dominance in the Dakota homeland of *Minisota Makoce*. Until spring
2006, text markers posted on the path to the fort explicitly stated
the opposite, "The soldiers were there to expel White settlers."
The Minnesota Historical Society had the audacity to suggest
that the purpose of the fort was to defend Indigenous interests,
rather than American expansion into Dakota homeland.[4]

Furthermore, the costumed guides who still welcome thousands of visitors to the fort every year as part of their living history program, depict a fort bustling with activity in the 1820s. It
is the place where tourists can "Enjoy the sights and sounds of
the past. Hear musket fire, the cannon's roar and the fife's shrill
tunes. Take part in the fort's everyday life. Shoulder a musket,
mend clothes, smell the stew, scrape a hide or sing along with
the soldiers. Take tea with Mrs. Snelling or sample the soldiers'
bread ration. Swing a hammer in the blacksmith shop or bar-
ter with the sutler—but remember that his store is the only one
for miles around!"[5] They best capture their romanticization of
the fort in the first paragraph of their brief history visible on
their Web site, "The story of Fort Snelling is the story of the
development of the U.S. Northwest. While surrounded today by
freeways and a large urban population, Fort Snelling was once a
lonely symbol of American ambition in the wilderness."[6] This is
the same kind of rhetoric characteristic of nineteenth-century
American expansionist propaganda. It reflects how little has
changed in 150 years.

What is missing in the analyses from both the Minnesota Historical Society and the University of Minnesota's American Indian
Studies department is a critical interrogation of the fort and what
it means in the context of Indigenous history. Rather than examining the fort as an army post for the United States military that
presaged the invasion and colonization of Dakota lands and the
extermination and ethnic cleansing of Dakota people, they depict
the fort as a benign presence in Minnesota that helped tame some

kind of wilderness. Any visitors to the current or renovated fort would not have to deal with the ugly issues of genocide, ethnic cleansing, or colonization. As Dakota people, we know the truth about that site has not been effectively told by the Minnesota Historical Society. Consequently, the Dakota people present at the February 9 meeting soundly rejected Child's plan. The only person other than Child and her students who publicly endorsed the project was the lone Anishinabe person appearing on the selected panel.[7]

If, however, we take a critical perspective, a different history of the area and the fort emerges. Let's take a look, for example, at the early history. In 1819, U.S. soldiers began construction of the fort, after the U.S. government offered a belated and only partial payment to the Dakota Oyate. They completed it in 1825. The MHS Web site on the fort, for example, acknowledges that Josiah's soldiers and officers "permanently changed the landscape" as they "made roads, built a gristmill and sawmill at St. Anthony Falls, planted hundreds of acres of vegetables, wheat and corn, cut hay for their livestock, felled trees for their fires, and made the first documented weather recordings in the area," all while they "enforced the laws and policies of the United States."[8] But, these are written about as though they are positive changes from the perspective of *Wasicu* Minnesotans. That perspective is implicit within the MHS narrative. It does not include the perspectives of Dakota people who witnessed the desecration and rape of our homeland, *Ina Maka*, the devastating diseases brought by *Wasicu* bodies, the eradication of Indigenous life forms in *Minisota Makoce* including the plants, animals, and people, or the overpowering influx of *Wasicu* masses into our homeland. From a critical perspective, the fort represents, first and foremost, American colonization of Indigenous people and lands. Thus, a dichotomy currently exists between the critical and non-critical perspectives. But, what would the moral perspective on the establishment of the fort be?

The Site of Genesis and Genocide

The history of the fort did not improve through the nineteenth century. As we know from the previous chapters, Fort Snelling was, most significantly, the concentration camp site where the U.S. government and White Minnesotans imprisoned our Dakota people, primarily women and children, during the winter of 1862–63. It was the site from which they sent Dakota and Ho-Chunk people on boats that went down the Mississippi River in spring 1863. And, it was the site where White soldiers hanged our leaders Medicine Bottle and Sakpe on November 11, 1865. In the latter part of the nineteenth century, the government used the fort as a training ground for American soldiers to participate in other campaigns and wars of imperialism against Indigenous Peoples, such as the Spanish-American War of 1898.

As Dakota people, we have two powerful interpretations of the site where Fort Snelling sits. We have the natural landscape that is important as the site of the Bdewakantunwan Dakota creation story relayed in chapter 1 and we have the man-made landscape that is one of absolute oppression. As Jim Anderson from the Bdote community has noted, the land there is the site of our genesis and our genocide. The place that gave birth to our Oyate is sacred ground; we consider it *wakan*. Yet, with the concentration camp and hanging of our leaders, it was also the site of one of the most egregious crimes that human beings can perpetrate on one another, that of genocide and ethnic cleansing.

In 2002 when the participants in the Dakota Commemorative March retraced the forced march from Lower Sioux to Fort Snelling, all of us poignantly felt the agony of walking toward the fort in the last few miles. I reflected on this experience and the experience of our ancestors in an article that appeared in the *American Indian Quarterly*'s special issue on the march: "The irony of having a United States military fort located on one of our most sacred sites would not have been lost on the women and children who made this march back in 1862. They, too, must have felt the love and power of this sacred land as they approached it on November 13, 1862. It must have been a source of strength, until they realized that this was where they would live and die in the coming months under cannons and within walls. The horror of a concentration camp imprisoning our own people on this sacred land hit me profoundly, marking me deeply as I made my way to the fort."[9]

As Dakota people, then, we face a strange and difficult dilemma. How do we pay homage to our history and the spirits of our ancestors at this site of genesis and genocide? If it were simply a site of genocide, and I am not using "simply" in a cavalier way, but instead to reflect a certain clarity rather than a complexity, then I think we could follow the example set at many other sites of genocide and develop a holocaust museum from the existing structures. The Auschwitz-Birkenau Memorial, for example, is toured by half a million people every year so they can experience the horror of the site where millions of Jews and other groups deemed undesirable by the Nazis were murdered during World War II. They have left the concentration camp structures intact while also developing a museum with exhibits and archives for educational purposes. The site stands as a monumental reminder of the horrific nature of genocide and inhumanity and a symbol of the Jewish Holocaust.

Fort Snelling carries such a stigma for Dakota people, albeit on a much smaller, but no less devastating scale than the Auschwitz site. Yet, to complicate the issue of genocide is this notion of sacred land, of *Bdote*, the Dakota Garden of Eden, if you will. If we, as Dakota people, could choose any future for our site of genesis, what might it look like? If we could break through the parameters of thought set by colonialism, would we choose to have a United States fort located on this sacred site with the American flag flying high? I do not believe any critical thinking Dakota person would want that. My guess is that, if we think deeply about this issue, we would prefer the land unburdened by the weight of a U.S. fort, a land returned to its original pristine condition, and a land under Dakota care that we could use for Dakota purposes.

The Minnesota Historical Society should create a Holocaust museum in Minnesota dedicated to educating the public about the genocide perpetrated against Dakota people. It would be an important reparative gesture. However, as long as that institution continues on its current trajectory and under its current leadership, I question their capacity to take on such an important and necessary task. Even amidst severe criticism from the Dakota community, the Minnesota Historical Society has thus proven itself incapable of presenting a critical view of the fort. In fact, the history of the site currently presented on their Web site does not even mention the concentration camp of 1862–63 or the hanging of Sakpe and Medicine Bottle. Even after Dakota people began publicly protesting the history presented at the site in 2006, the MHS did not alter their colonialist representations. The institution continues to refrain from using accurate terminology to describe the crimes against humanity perpetrated upon the Dakota, and it continues to present a benign narrative of Euro-American invasion and settlement. In essence, the MHS remains opposed to describing aspects of Minnesota's history that cast a dark shadow on the *Wasicu* settlers who have called our lands their home. Unless Dakota people were in complete control of such a facility, it is highly unlikely that the MHS would tell the shameful truth of Minnesota's history of genocide at that site.

Fort Snelling as a Fun-Filled Tourist Destination

The problems in interpretation at the Fort Snelling site hit home to me in the summer of 2006 when my daughter returned from Europe after attending a global youth leadership conference. While in Austria, she had the opportunity to visit Mauthausen, the last concentration camp freed by the Allied Forces during World War II. She told me, "Mom, you have to see the pictures

Mauthausen Concentration Camp, 2006. *Photo courtesy of Autumn Cavender-Wilson.*

of Mauthausen—it looks just like Fort Snelling." My fifteen year-old daughter was able to make a connection that most Minnesotans remain ignorant about. Not only that, she was amazed at how freely they presented the truth at the Mauthausen site, "not sugar-coating anything," in her words.

Both Mauthausen and Fort Snelling are concentration camp sites. Furthermore, they are both tourist attractions, though of a different sort to be sure. Mauthausen, like Auschwitz, is an educational site, a testament to the horror of genocide, committed to truth telling with the hope that people will never again commit such crimes against humanity. Even if the site prior to WW II had been used for additional purposes—that is, if it had additional uses besides that of a Nazi work/concentration camp—that narrative would not be allowed to dominate the interpretation because the larger story is far more significant. Fort Snelling, however, not only refrains from mentioning the concentration camp, hangings, genocide, and ethnic cleansing, thereby denying that history, it also actively promotes a celebratory narrative. For example, Historic Fort Snelling encourages tourism not to teach people about the dangers of White supremacy or colonialism, but to offer a place where White people can fulfill White fantasies. Interpreters dressed up in 1820s period costumes nos-

Fort Snelling
Concentration Camp, 2006.
Photo by Waziyatawin.

talgically relive a mythic past they help create while visitors to the site can walk away believing once again in the wholesomeness of manifest destiny ideology and American frontier settlement. The Minnesota Historical Society consistently reinforces that narrative with the programming they create.

For example, they regularly host a program called "Fort Kids: A Child's Work and Play at Historic Fort Snelling." In the summers, children can live out their Laura Ingalls Wilder fantasies as part of a day camp called "Little House in the Big Fort."[10] Perhaps the most shocking example of colonial myth making is the section "Especially for Kids" offered on their Web site. Minnesota parents are encouraged to host their children's birthday parties at Fort Snelling and the historical society offers special packages for such events. Can you imagine parents hosting a children's birthday party at Mauthausen? At Auschwitz? What Minnesota parents would want to celebrate their children's birthday at a concentration camp site? Such a proposition would violate the sensibilities of most Minnesotans, but most do not know the history. Thus, birthday celebrations will continue at Fort Snelling because the preeminent historical institution in the state chooses not to accurately relay this important, even defining, history of the site.

To be fair, it is important to discuss the changes in interpretation proposed by the Minnesota Historical Society as they seek to renovate the fort. Even MHS employees recognize the problematic and narrow interpretation that denied the dire consequences to Dakota people and froze their historical interpretation within the decade of the 1820s. Thus, within their proposals they now state they have "an obligation to help tell the full-range of stories necessary to convey the significance of this place for all Minnesotans, indeed for all Americans."[11] The MHS, then, will take a position similar to that of the Sesquicentennial Commission by attempting to provide a space to tell all stories relevant to the site, including "American settlement and the Louisiana Purchase, the role that Dred and Harriet Scott's presence in Minnesota played in precipitating the Civil War and the state's participation in the struggle . . . and the role of the Fort as a revived military base from the 1870s through World War II."[12] In this new interpretation, they will also give a few nods to Indigenous Peoples by relating the "experience of native peoples prior to European contact . . . the U.S.-Dakota Conflict of 1862 and subsequent military encounters with native people and their aftermaths."[13]

By now, all readers should notice the benign language they continue to use in discussing Indigenous topics. But, most important is the difficulty inherent in the notion of presenting competing narratives at the site. It is impossible to condemn genocide while also celebrating the ideology and institutions that would sanction and implement the perpetration of genocide. Similarly, Minnesotans cannot simultaneously condemn genocide while also continuing to celebrate what they gained from it. For Dakota people, it will be difficult to believe the institution's sincerity in condemning genocide while glorifying Little House frontier life and hosting birthday parties at the same time. This is not acceptable, just as it would not be acceptable to celebrate anything gained from the genocide perpetrated against the Jews.

Meanwhile, the MHS states they are committed to addressing the concerns of the Dakota community regarding this site
and they intend to recruit and employ members of our community as part of the interpretive planning process.[14] The MHS, as
an institution of colonialism, will thus put a few Dakota people
on the payroll to help sanction their project development. They
will reject the most critical Dakota voices and perspectives as
insignificant and the MHS will simply use their new Dakota employees as mouthpieces to express the MHS party line. What
will result will, at best, be an unsettling compromise of Dakota
integrity, or at worst, the total cooptation of Dakota individuals
to serve colonial interests. This divide and conquer tactic is an
example of colonialism at work. The MHS should not maintain
control over any sites central to the history of Dakota people,
nor should they be in charge of relating our history. We must
consider other options.

Paying Homage to Bdote's Deep History

What I am suggesting, as a way to pay homage to both the genesis and genocide that occurred at the *Bdote*/Fort Snelling site, is
the eradication of the fort. White Minnesotans could then work
to restore the site to a pristine condition and return the land
base to the Dakota Oyate. It is important for us to recognize
that for White Minnesotans the fort is probably the most significant symbol of American "settlement" and "progress" in this
state. For us it is a symbol of American imperialism. Thus, if we
were to take down the fort, it would compel White Minnesotans
to critically engage the shameful history of White invasion and
colonization. It would also be an important symbolic as well as
concrete victory in the Dakota quest for justice in our homeland.
The Upper Sioux Board of Trustees already passed a Community Resolution (No. 027-FY2006) supporting the campaign to
Take Down the Fort and to have the land returned in a pristine
condition to Dakota care and control.[15]

Before all you naysayers declare this impossible, let us imagine the possibility. Rather than devoting the $24.8 million the Minnesota Historical Society requested from the state legislature in 2008 to renovate (that is re-fortify the fort as a permanent icon of colonialism), a small portion of that could be reserved for demolition, cleanup, and an Indigenous planting project.[16] This would be an economically prudent use of Minnesota taxpayers' money because the desired end would be a fraction of the cost of renovation.

"But," critics would say, "the historic fort now serves an educational purpose for Minnesota's schoolchildren." Well, I've already discussed the poor education tourists receive at the fort and if education of *Wasicu* Minnesotans is the goal, wouldn't far more people be educated through a major campaign to take down the fort? Imagine the discussions that would emerge from such a campaign. Certainly, there would be those portions of the population who would adamantly defend the significance of the fort, and this would lead to a robust and provocative dialogue in a broad range of forums and media outlets. Not only could Minnesota's educators use this as a teaching tool in their classrooms, but newspapers, magazines, television and radio stations could also publicly address the topic. A campaign to "Take Down the Fort" would lead to unprecedented educational opportunities in the state of Minnesota regarding its historical past.

So rather than framing this issue as a loss of education for Minnesotans, strategically speaking, we need to frame the issue as a choice for White Minnesotans. Either Minnesotans can make the choice to re-invest consciously in this massive symbol of American imperialism, or they can consciously reject that symbol and decide that in the twenty-first century they do not want to continue participating in the ongoing colonization of *Minisota's* original people. If they choose to re-invest themselves in their imperialist symbol, Minnesotans would strip away all pretenses of a society free from oppression. They would remove the veil of Minnesota nice, revealing instead a colonizing society's ruthless

Take Down the Fort signs posted over Highway 5, 2006. *Photo by Waziyatawin.*

desire to keep up the business of colonizing. But, if Minnesotans consciously reject that symbol, then we have found allies with whom we can work toward creating a long-term sustainable way of living in Dakota homeland. We could work to create a place where Indigeneity is valued and respected.

Either way, such a sorting-out process would make us a stronger people. Imagine what a day of victory it would be for the Dakota Oyate as we watched the demolition of an icon of colonialism that settler society has imposed on our landscape for nearly 200 years. As the stone exploded and tumbled and the American flag fell, it would open up new possibilities for re-establishing Dakota self-determination in our homeland. Such a monumental victory would instill a whole new generation of our young people with incredible hope. Or if the fort is re-fortified and Minnesotans are willing to spend millions of dollars on such an effort, then more of us realize the magnitude of our work ahead and we mobilize a whole new generation of our young people for a long and needed struggle for liberation. We maintain our moral righteousness, having used reason and logic to attempt to compel White Minnesotans to do the right thing, and if they fail, we work to compel change using other means.

The Importance of Symbols

Americans clearly understand the importance of symbols to nations of people. When we invaded Iraq in 2003, the United States government helped to institute a de-Baathification of Iraq so they could eliminate the influence of Saddam Hussein's Arab Baath Socialist Party. Americans cheered when, with the help of the U.S. marines, the Iraqi civilians toppled a statue of Saddam Hussein in the capital's Firdos Square on Wednesday, April 9, 2003. It was precisely because Americans understood the power of symbols that it was a U.S. Marine–armored recovery wagon that pulled the statue down and dragged it through the streets of Baghdad.

American popular imagination has also created a place for the toppling of iconic images that violate principles of freedom and justice. In the 2006 Hollywood sci-fi blockbuster *V for Vendetta*, our sympathy as moviegoers was squarely with V who was a revolutionary freedom fighter, battling a fictitious totalitarian regime that had overwhelmed Great Britain. Evey, the female protagonist played by Natalie Portman, asks V, "You really think that blowing up parliament is going to make this country a better place?" V replied, "There is no certainty, only opportunity." He then went on to remark, "The building is a symbol, as is the act of destroying it. Symbols, given power by people. Alone, the symbol is meaningless but with enough people, blowing up a building can change the world." In the end when they blow British Parliament to smithereens, the audience cheers this symbolic victory.

If we similarly invest in the demolition of Fort Snelling as a symbol of the Dakota reclamation of our homeland, then when we take down the fort, we will be setting ourselves on a new course of history, a course toward liberation. We can seek to honor our ancestors by reclaiming what settler society forcibly took from us. We can work to restore dignity to the land and our dignity as human beings. We can transform the pain of our past into strength for our future and work toward strategic and revolutionary change. All of this is only possible, however, if we first embrace the tragedy in our past and allow ourselves to imagine a different future.

Metaphorically Dismantling the Fort

The struggle does not end there, however. Fort Snelling is a symbol for all the icons of imperialism and colonialism that currently mark our landscape. Fort Snelling is a symbol for the ideology that supports the subjugation and oppression of Peoples. Fort Snelling is a symbol of dominance imposed on the landscape. Still, Fort Snelling is only one of the symbols requiring eradication.

If we recognize that colonialism is a crime against humanity, just as genocide and ethnic cleansing are crimes against humanity, all our symbols need to reflect those values. Similar to the way Europe underwent a program of de-Nazification after World War II, so too must Minnesota cease to support all ideological and material monikers that ask us to celebrate the acts we condemn. This process will require all of us to engage in a statewide inventory of the symbols that currently exist unchallenged. That is, we must *Take Down the Fort* wherever it exists.

For example, White Minnesotans still celebrate the perpetrators of Dakota genocide. Apologists for the perpetrators insist that they are merely complex people with good and bad traits.[17] Yet, we do not accept such assessments of Adolf Hitler or Adolf Eichmann. While no human being is all "evil," we generally do not sing the praises of perpetrators of heinous crimes against humanity because they possess a few positive attributes or perform a few positive actions . . . unless they are perpetrators of heinous crimes against Indigenous Peoples. Thus, Minnesotans still celebrate the architect of Minnesota's genocidal and ethnic cleansing policies against the Dakota, Alexander Ramsey. Minnesotans still celebrate Henry Sibley, who implemented Ramsey's plan. Not only are their crimes against humanity ignored or dismissed as inconsequential by the public, Minnesotans continue to praise them as noble and righteous founding fathers of a beloved state. Minnesotans have etched their memory in the landscape to remind us every day that they are beloved historical figures. We have counties named after them, roads, streets, parks, and even schools bearing their names. Yet, the double standards White Minnesotans maintain are clearly illuminated when we ask the questions: What would we say about a society that still celebrated their perpetrators of genocide and ethnic cleansing? Would Minnesotans allow their children to attend schools named in honor of Hitler or Eichmann, or what about the likes of Stalin or Milosevic?

In fact, as Minnesota celebrates its 150th year of statehood, Minnesotans remind us that very little has changed in the mindset of some residents since the nineteenth century. The Minnesota Historical Society is sponsoring the exhibit "MN150: The People, Places, and Things That Shape Our State," and while Ramsey did not make the MN150 List, Sibley did. Lois Glewwe of South St. Paul submitted the winning nomination that allowed Henry Hastings Sibley to make the list. It reads:

> Henry Sibley's personality, beliefs, intelligence, and ability were a great influence on what Minnesota became. It was the strength of his character that set the tone for how Minnesota would behave as a state—how we would treat those who lived here before us, what we should value in a politician, and what kind of expectations we should have for our citizenry. Sibley was an example of the kind of somewhat pragmatic but almost charismatic personality who was in the right place at the right time to bring a sense or [sic] order, righteousness, and permanence to a volatile community. In many ways he

set the stage for Minnesota to produce personalities that
are part outdoorsman, part statesman, part soldier, part
preacher, part family man, part cad, part introvert, and
part motivator. Although his actions have not produced
anything close to an umblemished [sic] record in terms
of fairness to any constituency, he remains an example
of what Minnesota expects of its leaders.[18]

Nineteenth-century Minnesotans could have written this same
biographical statement. One thing that Glewwe and I would
agree on is that Sibley did set the tone for how the state would
behave. However, Dakota people do not honor him for it. It is
unfortunate that Minnesotans continue to idealize Ramsey's
first-hand man in the ethnic cleansing campaigns against the
Dakota. This is precisely what needs to change.

It is time that all Minnesotans begin to contemplate how
their celebrations and glorifications of horrific people and acts
affect Dakota people. The messages, either implicitly or explicitly conveyed to us, are that we are expendable human beings
and that our suffering is acceptable as long as White Minnesotans benefit. White Minnesotans are telling us that genocide
is okay, as long as White Minnesotans benefited from it. They
are telling us that ethnic cleansing is okay, as long as White Minnesotans benefited from it. They are telling us that might is right
and that White is right.

For example, in the town of Redwood Falls, located next to
the Lower Sioux Reservation, there is a municipal park named
after Alexander Ramsey. As I have written elsewhere, "Almost
every day of their lives, Dakota people at Lower Sioux are re-
minded that Minnesota loves the man who called for the extermination of our People. This would not happen in a place free
from oppression."[19] Again, to illuminate the double standard, can
you imagine Jews living adjacent to a municipal park named after Hitler? It is outrageous that in the twenty-first century White
Minnesotans are still forcing Dakota people to live amidst such

blatant anti-Indian expression within our own homeland. Yet, most White Minnesotans never give any thought as to how their glorifications continue a centuries-long assault on Dakota humanity.

Furthermore, the assaults continue not just in terms of the celebration of genocide and ethnic cleansing; they also continue in the total denial of wrongdoing in regards to the land. As Mohawk scholar Taiaiake Alfred declares, "The perpetrators know it is wrong to steal a country and to deny it is a crime."[20] What moral positioning allows for the massive theft of a People's homeland? What moral positioning allows for the ongoing denial of that homeland to the Original People? If one attempts to justify such theft, the racism and colonialism quickly become apparent. Theft of a homeland can only be justified through the dehumanization of the original occupiers. It can only be justified through a self-declaration of superiority by the thieves. In the twenty-first century, we should not tolerate that kind of justification—it is not just Dakota people who should not tolerate it; no Minnesotan should tolerate it.

Thus, our task is to eliminate the projects in the state that continue to celebrate all that was gained at Indigenous expense and everything that serves to rationalize genocide, ethnic cleansing, land theft, and colonization. It is time to take down all the forts, literally and metaphorically. This is not an unreasonable expectation if we are attempting to create a just society. A just society simply would not tolerate such icons of colonialism.

Notes

1. See www.mnhs.org/places/sites/hfs/tour/tour.html (accessed January 9, 2008).

2. http://www.mnhs.org/places/sites/hfs/map/fortrest.html (accessed January 9, 2008).

3. See the proposed plan produced by the American Indian Studies Department at the University of Minnesota, "Bdote Where the Riv-

ers Meet: Developing a Center for Dakota Iapi and Ojibwemowin at Fort Snelling," page 6, circulated in 2005–2006.

4. This statement was on a text marker with the heading, "Were the soldiers here to protect White settlers?" I took a photograph of this and other text markers in April 2006 on a visit to Minnesota and by the time I returned in July of that year, the Minnesota Historical Society had removed those markers. Photographs are in author's collection.

5. See http://www.mnhs.org/places/sites/hfs/visiting.html (accessed April 3, 2006).

6. See http://www.mnhs.org/places/sites/hfs/history.html (accessed April 3, 2006).

7. Unfortunately, even after the plan was publicly rejected by Dakota people, Child and her students continued to promote this plan, publicly presenting on it as late as April 2007 as part of a conference entitled, "Heritage Sites/Political Spaces: Rethinking Belonging," held at the University of Minnesota. Her disregard for Dakota concerns about her plan violates numerous academic standards concerning professional research ethics. Ironically, when an audience member at this April 2007 forum asked her and her student what they thought about the *Take Down the Fort* campaign, they both responded that it was wonderful, but that it wasn't going to happen because it was unrealistic. Her solution, then, is to sell out a larger vision so she can settle for smaller scraps. The American Indian Studies program at the University of Minnesota remains unwilling to acknowledge the problems associated with their handling of this project. The interim chair, Jean O'Brien, has refused to meet to discuss this and other issues concerning Dakota truth telling.

8. See http://www.mnhs.org/places/sites/hfs/history.html (accessed April 3, 2006).

9. See Waziyatawin Angela Wilson, "A Journey of Healing and Awakening," in *American Indian Quarterly* 28, no. 2 (Winter/Spring 2004): 280 and the reprinted chapter in Waziyatawin Angela Wilson, ed., *In the Footsteps of Our Ancestors: The Dakota Commemorative Marches of the 21ˢᵗ Century* (St. Paul: Living Justice Press, 2006).

10. For a critique of the colonialism and racism inherent in the writing of Laura Ingalls Wilder and the implications of her work for contemporary Indigenous Peoples, see Waziyatawin Angela Wilson,

"Burning Down the House: Laura Ingalls Wilder and American Colonialism," in Don Jacobs, ed., *Unlearning the Language of Conquest: Scholars Expose Anti-Indianism in America* (Austin: University of Texas Press, 2006), 66–80.

11. See "New Visitor Center at Fort Snelling: Documentation for Consultation," submitted by the Minnesota Historical Society in support of the Section 106 Review of the Historic Fort Snelling Visitor Center and Revitalization Project," August 30, 2007.

12. Ibid., 24.

13. Ibid., 24.

14. Ibid., 43.

15. This Upper Sioux Community Resolution was passed unanimously by the Board of Trustees on June 20, 2006.

16. $24.8 million is the amount requested for the 2008 legislative session. The initial request was $22.6 million for the 2006 legislative session. The MHS sent out requests to "friends" of the institution to solicit help in achieving political support for their renovations.

17. For example, longtime Minnesota Historical Society employee and author of a biography of Sibley, Rhoda Gilman, still maintains such an argument.

18. See http://discovery.mnhs.org/MN150/index.php?title= Henry_Hastings_Sibley.

19. Wilson, ed., *In the Footsteps of Our Ancestors*, 62.

20. Taiaiake Alfred, "Warrior Scholarship: Seeing the University as a Ground of Contention," in Devon Mihesuah and Angela Wilson, eds., *Indigenizing the Academy: Transforming Scholarship and Empowering Communities* (Lincoln: University of Nebraska Press, 2004), 90–91.

FOUR

Just Short of Breaking Camp

Justice is reclaiming our humanity by reclaiming our sacred earth—that earth is our homeland.

— GABRIELLE TATEYUSKANSKAN

Taking Down the Fort, as essential as it is, is not enough to create a just society. Furthermore, it is not enough to make restitution for the crimes of genocide, ethnic cleansing, and colonization. Even if all other oppression against Dakota people were to cease today, as long as Minnesotans continue to deny us basic access to and freedoms in our homeland, gross injustices will continue. Thus, for the dominant society to address the historical and contemporary harms perpetrated against the Dakota people, they must take additional actions.

In a conversation with Melvin Grey Owl, an elder from the Crow Creek reservation in South Dakota, in the summer of 2007, he conveyed a story about an interview he gave a few years ago in Cleveland. The interviewer had offered him the last words of the day and he took the opportunity to tell her, and the audience that would be listening, about his vision for the future. He told all the *Wasicu*s that it was time for them to break camp, to saddle up their horses, drive to the coast, load themselves onto boats, and go back home. Though he was supposed to have the last word of the interview, somehow they never played his message.

Most Indigenous Peoples can relate to Grey Owl's perspective. Indeed, there is a widespread belief in Indigenous communities that we would be much better off if all the invaders would just go home. There remain many jokes in Indian country about the loose immigration policies of our ancestors and many dream of what life was like prior to invasion.

While we all might imagine a future in which invaders have gone home, I would suggest that what we need to consider more seriously is a solution just short of breaking camp. We recognize that our lives are now intertwined with the non-Indigenous world to such an extent that breaking camp is not a position we can publicly advocate. This chapter will explore an alternative that is radical, but that allows settlers and Indigenous Peoples to co-create the foundation for a just, sustainable, and respectful society.

Among Dakota people, the extent of colonization has disallowed most of our people from even imagining a reality in which Minnesotans might address outstanding issues of injustice. Thus, we continue to fight for scraps off the master's table, and many have even agreed to disavow their Dakota identity to achieve what represents some semblance of justice in their own eyes. We need an alternative vision. This chapter will explore an alternative vision, but first, it will consider the current options on the table for Dakota people.

Options on the Table

One option, of course, is to do nothing. This is the easiest option. Or, we could continue to plug along, attempting to negotiate the best deal we can from the hands we are dealt. We could continue to fight smaller battles within the current legal system, we could continue to depend on gaming as a source of revenue, and we could continue to use a Band-Aid approach to resolve our monumental social problems.

Several years ago, another group formed a nonprofit organization to reclaim the land bases and economic privileges they felt were unfairly dispensed by the United States government to the wrong people. They are the Minnesota Mdewakanton Dakota Oyate who organized at Lower Sioux in 2004 where they elected leaders and drafted a constitution they hoped would "provide a meaningful system for governance as well as offer a design for long-term political stability."[1] In 1888, 1889, and 1890, Congress appropriated funds for the exclusive use of the Mdewakanton Dakota people who were loyal to the United States government during the U.S.–Dakota War of 1862. That is, the U.S. government rewarded those Dakota people (who sided with the Whites against other Dakota people) with land bases in southern Minnesota. Those Dakota people are lineally descended from the "loyal Mdewakanton" of the nineteenth century. They want the designated lands and the trust assets promised to their ancestors. They argue that the U.S. breached its fiduciary duty to the "loyal Mdewakanton" by allowing the transfer of trust assets (including casino profits) to the wrong parties. They want to lay claim to the Lower Sioux, Prior Lake, and Prairie Island lands and assets, or else receive just compensation from the United States government. Given the popularity of this option among Dakota people, it is a current strategy for land reclamation that we must discuss. Approximately 7,500 Dakota people have signed on to this lawsuit and many more thousands have tried.

Rekindling Colonialism's Factions

One of the most insidious characteristics of colonialism is the way in which it divides the colonized. Of course, colonialism is not an abstract force that creates profound and lasting divisions on its own. Instead, real people work to systematically divide and conquer the people they hope to subjugate. Thus, in the case of Dakota people, we can look back at the White populations who invaded Minnesota in the first half of the nineteenth century as the original culprits of a divide and conquer policy perpetrated against us. The early missionaries, Indian agents, soldiers, traders, and settlers all worked to favor Dakota people compliant to their wishes and to pit them against the Dakota people who were resistant to invasion and oppression. For example, Indian

Agent Thomas J. Galbraith wrote in 1861 about conditions at the agency prior to the war: "By my predecessor a new and radical system was inaugurated, and in its inauguration he was aided by the Christian missionaries and by the government. The treaties of 1858 were ostensibly made to carry this new system into effect. The theory, in substance, was to break up the community system which obtained among the Sioux, weaken and destroy their tribal relations, and individualize them, by giving each of them a separate home."[2] This was not a new practice in the nineteenth century and it has proven to be a successful imperial enterprise in the twenty-first century. Eventually these colonial divisions become embedded within our communities. As colonized people, we then carry out our prescribed positions and activities with only a nudge from colonizer society.

The lawsuit (Sheldon Peters Wolfchild, Ernie Peters Long-walker, Scott Adolphson, Morris J. Pendleton, Barbara Feezor Buttes, et al. vs. United States, Case No. 03-2684-L) filed on behalf of the "loyal Mdewakanton," for example, has revived in a very public way the old factions between the "cut-hair" or "friendly" Dakota and the "blanket" or "hostile" Dakota. Interestingly, these were not always clear distinctions prior to the U.S.–Dakota War of 1862. For instance, the leader of resistance in 1862—Taoyateduta (His Red Nation), also known as Kangi Cistinna (Little Crow)—had received educational training from missionaries and attended church services in the years leading up to the war, activities usually associated with the "cut-hairs." However, when the war broke out, most Dakota people were required to make a conscious choice regarding which side they were willing to stake their lives. In that context, Taoyateduta and his fellow resistors chose to fight the *Wasicu* invaders while others sought to use the opportunity to curry favor with the *Wasicu* invaders by either protecting them or by taking up arms against their resisting Dakota relatives. In some cases, the traitors of Dakota people were mixed bloods with family on both sides of the war (such as the LaFramboise, Frenier, and Renville families);

Lynching of Medicine Bottle and Sakpe, November 11, 1865. *Courtesy of the Minnesota Historical Society.*

in other cases they were full-blooded Dakota people (such as Wabasha and Taopi) who believed that in siding with the invaders, they would ensure a better life for their families and future generations.

Ironically, Sheldon Wolfchild, who has become the spokesperson for the "loyal Mdewakanton" lawsuit, frequently invokes his ancestor Wakan Ozanzan (Medicine Bottle) who was one of the leaders hanged on November 11, 1865, for his resistance to Whites in the 1862 war. Saying, "Medicine Bottle fought back. Now I am too," Wolfchild desires to carry his ancestor's spirit of resistance into his current efforts for Dakota people.[3] This stated position is wildly inconsistent with the aims of the lawsuit, however. While extolling posthumously Medicine Bottle's actions in defense of our people, lands, and way of life, Wolfchild has not been able to continue that agenda in his own vision for the future, as he is now publicly declaring his loyalty to the U.S., not to Dakota people. In 1862, Medicine Bottle fought against those whom the U.S. government would identify as the "loyal Mdewakanton."

Disavowal of Dakota Identity as a Pathway to Justice

According to the claim filed by Wolfchild and others in 2004, the "loyal Mdewakanton formed a contract with the United States in which they agreed to sever their tribal relations, express loyalty to the United States, and move onto the 1886 lands. In exchange, the United States would purchase the 1886 lands and place them in trust for the Mdewakanton."[4] Thus, the censuses created out of those negotiations record the names of those Dakota individuals willing to sever their tribal relations. Given the importance of kinship among Dakota people, this is nothing less than the disavowal of Dakota identity.

Now, generations later, the descendants of those who severed tribal ties are claiming they have a superior right to lands in Dakota homeland that supersedes the rights of other Dakota people, some of whom have been living on the contested parcels long before there was gaming and the opportunity for wealth. Most outsiders to the lawsuit cannot help but believe the lawsuit is about acquiring Shakopee's wealth and that with dollar signs in their eyes, the 7,500 claimants are hoping to gain their piece of that large economic pie. In the meantime, numerous questions remain about their legal claims to the Bdewakantunwan reservations in Minnesota and the U.S. colonial court system will likely not make any final determinations for years.

Most troubling, however, is the notion that these Dakota people believe our strongest claim to our homeland comes from denying who we are as Dakota people. What is so startling is that rather than challenging the colonial system that serves to oppress all Dakota people and deny us access to and justice in our homeland, so many Dakota people are willing to celebrate their legacy of loyalty to the United States government. Given the fact that it was the United States government and its citizens that deprived us of our freedom (and instead worked toward our extermination, ethnic cleansing, and brutal subjugation), attesting loyalty to such a government is the ultimate testament to the extent of our colonization.

Even if the claimants win their lawsuit, what do they win? The right to a land base so small it would not likely accommodate all 7,500 families? The right to casinos in the Twin Cities metropolitan area? The right to declare their loyalty once again to a government that not only continues to oppress us, but also continues its imperialistic endeavors in all corners of the globe? Yikes. Even the best-case scenario in the lawsuit is shortsighted and highly problematic. Furthermore, as Kanien'kehaka scholar Taiaiake Alfred points out, pursuing Indigenous empowerment through economic development and gaming only mimics the logic of the colonizers, "The implication of the economic development approach is integration into the consumer culture of mainstream capitalist society, which is the defeat of the possibility of ways of life associated with Onkwehonwe [Original People] cultures."[5] The strategies we use to seek empowerment, then, must be in accordance with Dakota ethics if they are going to assist us in reclaiming Dakota ways of being. With this in mind, it is hard to justify the lawsuit as a strategy of Dakota empowerment.

The strategy employed by the lawsuit is, moreover, inconsistent with other actions by some of the claimants who might otherwise engage projects that support and encourage Dakota cultural traditions and ways of being. For example, Sheldon Wolfchild has also coordinated memorial horse rides in honor of the thirty-eight hanged at Mankato in 1862 and the two hanged at Fort Snelling in 1865. While he may not espouse an accompanying critical rhetoric about what happened in 1862, the act of honoring Dakota men sentenced to execution for their crimes against White people is certainly a subversive act in a colonial context. Dakota honoring of those men means reconfiguring them in the historical imagination as heroes, martyrs, and Dakota patriots, rather than their characterization by White society as murderers, rapists, and thieves. This example complicates the easy characterization of all those who signed on to the lawsuit as truly "loyal" to the U.S. and it illuminates the inconsistent nature of their positioning.

Furthermore, the willingness of so many people with this "loyal Mdewakanton" Dakota ancestry to sign on to the lawsuit has reinvigorated colonialism's factions and the resulting pain and strife is apparent, especially at Lower Sioux. Dakota people do not usually frame the debate today as one between the "cut-hairs" and "blanket" Dakota, but we frame it as a struggle between those who have signed on to the lawsuit and those who have not. Lower Sioux elder Maude Bluestone described how the lawsuit has cut like a knife through the Mdewakanton Dakota, creating "so much hatred."[6] Consequently, Lower Sioux has experienced tremendous turmoil over the matter that has erupted in internal, intratribal protests, increased political instability, threats of violence, and even arson to tribal facilities. All of these have the potential to lead to years of political unrest and the festering of mutual animosity between the factions.

Just as the lawsuit claimants have publicly declared their ongoing allegiance to the U.S., others are just as committed to an ongoing resistance to colonialism and a celebration of Dakota patriots. For example, Santee tribal members such as Roger Trudell and Kalon Strickland have expressed their pride in being descended from those who resisted invasion and colonization. Trudell captured the crux of the issue stating, "The whole thing diminishes us as a people. We're the real Mdewakanton. The ones who stayed in Minnesota renounced their tribalism."[7] Strickland similarly asserted, "We're the bad Indians. We're the ones who fought."[8] Inherent in Trudell's and Strickland's comments are the notions that those who have the real claim to Minnesota are those who fought to defend it and those who never severed their tribal ties. From that moral perspective, the ones who make their claim to land based upon a contract with the colonizer government for their betrayal of their own people is less legitimate. This position resonates with many other Dakota people who see the lawsuit as a troubling means to an even more troubling end, initiated by those with the least moral claim to the land.

Frankly, traitors and sellouts are not inspiring. Because Dakota people fought and died to defend our lands and way of life, we cannot hold up as admirable anyone who opposed that project, thereby assisting White colonizer society in dispossessing us from our lands and carrying out policies of genocide. It is quite typical for Dakota individuals to possess ancestors who fought on both sides of the war, who both fled and were forcibly removed, and who were hanged or imprisoned. Furthermore, many of us can recognize that all of our ancestors believed they were making the best choices they could under horrendous circumstances and that the real perpetrators of injustices were the invading populations to Dakota homeland. Nonetheless, today we not only must decide who is worthy of celebration and whose legacy we want to uphold, we must also decide whose actions we want to emulate.

Let us invoke the leadership of Wakan Ozanzan and Taoyateduta, but let us carry their spirit of resistance to everything we do. Let us remember that the colonizers killed them because they fought to defend our lands and way of life. I do not for a moment believe they sacrificed their lives so their future descendants and Dakota relatives could declare their allegiance to the government and the society that killed them.

A Broader Vision of Justice for Dakota People

Let us, then, consider additional options—ones that have not been publicly engaged in any serious way. In order to articulate a broader vision of justice for Dakota people, we must first examine the grounds on which we would make a claim for justice.

First, our claim to *Minisota Makoce* is that of heirs to the ancient homeland of our Oyate. This land is our inheritance and it belongs to all Dakota people, not just the Bdewakantunwan, loyal or not. What sets this claim apart from the "loyal Mdewakanton" lawsuit is that this inherent right is based on our conception of ourselves as Dakota people, not on a disavowal of our indigeneity. Thus, what would emerge from a successful claim would be the reinforcement of the core values and worldview that make the Dakota Oyate a distinct entity.

Second, I would argue that because of the brutal way in which Minnesotans and the United States government exterminated us and dispossessed us of our lands, they have an obligation to make reparations. The crimes against Dakota people did not end in the nineteenth century, nor did they end in the twentieth century. They continue right up to the present moment through the ongoing denial of justice to Dakota people. So the question is: What does recognition of genocide, ethnic cleansing, and colonization demand?

This issue marks the point at which discussions between Dakota people and *Wasicu* people usually break down. During the first Dakota Commemorative March, a group of White supporters wanted to show solidarity with our marchers by walking with us for a few miles through the town of New Ulm. One of the men, eager to hear more about why we were engaged in the Commemorative March, initiated a discussion with me about Dakota-White relations. He explained to me that many of the people in New Ulm were still racist, but that he was part of a group that was not. In fact, as proof he told me he had worked to bring in Dakota dancers, a youth group from Lower Sioux, to perform for New Ulm's townspeople during their Oktoberfest celebration. As I was envisioning Dakota youth dancing in front of beer-drinking Whites for their entertainment, I attempted to explain to the man why that was not a satisfactory example of developing good relations with Dakota people. Calling out a need for justice before we can live in peaceful co-existence, I could see him growing increasingly nervous. Finally he said with a small laugh, "What do you want, the land back?" After that conversation, we never saw him again.

This example illuminates that even seemingly supportive White Minnesotans want good relations with Dakota people, but only if they can maintain the status quo. Many of them really want us to feel good about White people, to be friendly toward White people, and even admire White people, but they avoid the issue of justice like the plague. While a few Dakota people may accept token gestures of friendliness by Whites as sufficient to right all historical harms, Whites do not persuade most Dakota people so easily. Instead, there is an ongoing resentment and distrust toward the White occupiers of our homeland because we recognize the emptiness of small gestures that do not jeopardize the existing social order. We hunger for something much, much greater.

If Minnesotans today accept the premises that this is the ancestral land of the Dakota Oyate and that settler society perpetrated tremendous crimes against us so that they could dispossess us of our lands and resources, then it is only logical that such recognition would demand concrete action to repair these wrongs. What might that look like?

The Ute Example

Because the colonization process has so thoroughly indoctrinated all of us with ideas regarding the fixed state of affairs (the U.S. will not change, it is a lasting entity, capitalism is a superior economic system, there is nothing we can do about injustice, etc.), most of us never dare to dream about what a just society might look like. Even while I have actively worked toward the decolonization of my own mind, the limitations of my thinking still shock me at times. I had such an experience a few summers ago when my husband and I were traveling a leisurely scenic route from Minnesota to Arizona. After traveling through hundreds of miles of stunningly beautiful national forest lands, we had stopped in the town of Ouray, Colorado, nicknamed the "Switzerland of America." Taking the name from a chief of the Uncompahgre Band of Utes in the late nineteenth century, White settlers established the town of Ouray in 1876. Today, Americans prize Ouray for its therapeutic hot springs and spectacular mountain scenery. We enjoyed our time in Ouray, made use of the hot springs, but all the while wondered whether the Ute people still maintained any access to their ancestral lands.

We left there and continued to travel southwest toward the four corners region. It was then we realized that at least some of the Utes, the Weeminuche Band, ended up in an extraordinarily barren, high desert section of southwestern Colorado, while the United States government sent most of the other Ute groups to the Uintah Reservation in Utah. It must have seemed like the moon to the heartbroken Utes. It seemed incomprehensible to me that with all the vast stretches of national forest wilderness existing in their former homelands, the Utes continued to be denied even a portion of those lands.

The Ute story is astonishingly similar to the Dakota story. After negotiating a treaty in 1868 that theoretically guaranteed their land title forever, Whites discovered resources (gold and silver) in the San Juan Mountains and began clamoring for Ute land. The government pressured the Utes to become full-time farmers as part of their assimilation campaign and this served to create factionalism among them. Annuities guaranteed by treaty were late and conflicts with Indian Agent Nathan Meeker led to an unjustified military intervention by government forces and a resulting military engagement. The Utes responsible for killing White invaders and for holding White women as hostages consequently faced federal charges and military trial. Meanwhile, White settlers called for the removal of Utes from Colorado. In 1881, government soldiers moved the Utes out of their ancestral lands at gunpoint.[9]

More than a century later when hundreds of Ute people gathered in 1993 to erect a monument commemorating the Battle of

Milk Creek in their former lands, Ute spokesperson Luke Duncan remarked, "We were removed to a country not our own. We still feel that loss today. It was very cruel."[10] It remains a crime against humanity to deny that land to Ute people while the San Juan Public Lands alone encompass 2.5 million acres and other national forests and parks in Colorado claim millions more acres of land. The story is the same here in Minnesota, but my eyes were not open to this reality until I recognized the injustices experienced by another Indigenous Nation.

Land Reparations

Historian Andrea Smith argues that as Indigenous Peoples consider the issue of reparations (along with African American reparations activists) that we do so as a "radical demand for social transformation."[11] That is, rather than seeking monetary compensation dispensed to individuals that would only serve to reinforce institutionalized structures of White supremacy, for example, we should instead seek an outcome that would challenge the oppressive economic system. Land reparations offer one way to address that issue while also calling attention to the wealth Whites still obtain from Dakota homeland.

Before readers dismiss this option out of hand, let me point out that land reparations need not involve divesting White people of their private land holdings. In the state of Minnesota, for example, about 22 percent of the total land area is identified as "public land." This includes federal agency lands, state agency lands, tax-forfeited lands, and metro-commissioned lands totaling 11,836,375 acres.[12] That means Minnesotans and the federal government could return nearly twelve million acres of land to Dakota people tomorrow without touching a single acre of privately held land.

We can make the case for Dakota land return on a couple of different grounds. First, the Canadian example of Nunavut offers a possible model for proceeding with Dakota land reparations. In

1976, the Inuit Tapirisat of Canada (ITC) proposed the creation of Nunavut Territory "as part of a comprehensive settlement of Inuit land claims in the Northwest Territories."[13] After years of planning and preparation, the Nunavut Territory and Government came into existence on April 1, 1999. In the "Agreement Between the Inuit of the Nunavut Settlement Area and Her Majesty The Queen in Right of Canada," the Inuit represented by the Tungavik Federation of Nunavut asserted their claim based on their "traditional and current use and occupation of the lands, waters and land-fast ice therein in accordance with their own customs and usages."[14] This has not been an uncomplicated or easy process and, certainly, the Government of Nunavut is still fraught with problems they are working to resolve, but the notion of a territory creation to address outstanding land claims is one worth considering in the U.S. That land claim was based on an ancient and historic relationship the Inuits have with that land base, just as the Dakota claim would be based on our ancient and historic relationship with *Minisota Makoce*.

Dakota people can make land claims on another basis, however, and that is the need of a diasporic people to reunite in their homeland. This is a claim that the United States has consistently supported in the case of Israel, as a homeland for the Jews. Long before the state of Israel was created, Theodor Herzl (among others in the Zionist movement), argued the need for the creation of a Jewish State not only as a means to end the persecution regularly faced by Jews as they lived amidst host countries throughout the world, but also as a means to consolidate the population and flourish as a people. Herzl argued that the "creation of a new State is neither ridiculous nor impossible." He was right.

The State of Israel officially came into existence in 1948, after the Zionist movement began to gain international support, as evidenced first in Great Britain's Balfour Declaration in 1917. The Balfour Declaration publicly supported the establishment of a Jewish state in Palestine. After World War I, the League of

Nations in 1922 also included the mandate for Palestine. Jewish migration to Palestine was under way long before 1948 and settlement and development of the area grew with increasing international support. Jewish demands for a separate state then dramatically increased before and during World War II because of the brutal extermination policies implemented under the Nazis. As Great Britain attempted to maintain a balance between the Jewish community and Palestine's Arab population, this increasingly put them at odds with Jews seeking freedom from limits on Jewish immigration to Palestine. This resulted in a conflicted relationship between the Jewish community and Great Britain. The United Nations intervened by adopting a plan that would divide Palestine into Jewish and Arab states in 1947, sending 700,000 Arab Palestinians into flight and triggering an Arab military response. The following year, in the midst of the first Arab-Israeli war, Israel declared its independence.[15]

We can trace U.S. support for the establishment of a Jewish state at least back to the presidency of Woodrow Wilson and the time of the Balfour Declaration. Subsequent presidents continued U.S. support. In 1922, the U.S. Congress passed Joint Resolution 322, "That the United States of American favors the establishment of a national home for the Jewish people, it being clearly understood that nothing shall be done which may prejudice the civil and religious rights of Christian and all other non-Jewish communities in Palestine, and that the holy places and religious buildings and sites in Palestine be adequately protected." Even before President Harry Truman took office, he clearly connected the Jewish persecution under the Nazis with the need for a Jewish state, declaring at a Chicago rally, "Today, not tomorrow, we must do all that is humanly possible to provide a haven for all those who can be grasped from the hands of Nazi butchers. Free lands must be opened to them."[16] Once he was in the presidential office, Truman initiated several studies on the situation in Palestine and reconfirmed his position that because of Jewish persecution, the Jews needed a homeland. The

U.S. supported the UN resolution for a division of Palestine and Truman publicly announced U.S. support for the Israelis immediately after their declaration of statehood.[17] Since its establishment, U.S. policy has continued to support Israel and to protect the security of the Jewish homeland.

In fact, the U.S. remains the largest bilateral donor to Israel. According to USAID, "The close bilateral relationship that the United States has with Israel serves the national security interests of both countries. The Government of Israel's (GOI) political and economic stability continues to be a key objective of U.S. foreign policy in the Middle East." This commitment to Israel is most readily evident in the money the U.S. continues to pour into Israel. In fiscal year 2006 alone, USAID to Israel was $240,000,000, lowered from $357,120,000 in 2005 and $477,168,000 in 2004.[18] The Washington Report on Middle East Affairs states that the grand total of "Benefits to Israel of U.S. Aid Since 1949" is $84,854,827,200.[19] Not only did the U.S. support the establishment of Jewish State, it also continues to support it financially.

Obviously, the state of ongoing crisis in the Middle East, with the Israel-Palestinian conflict still raging, indicates that populations will not achieve a state of peaceful co-existence when one population is removed from their lands to create a new political entity. The Palestinians, clearly, have suffered unjustly because of the creation of Israel and the ongoing encroachment of Israeli settlements into contested Arab territories. Just such a removal policy perpetrated against the Dakota population in Minnesota has meant years of suffering for Dakota people and the impossibility of achieving peaceful relations until Dakota people achieve justice. Similarly, we would undermine the possibility of peaceful co-existence by forcibly removing White people and other non-Dakota populations to make way for returning Dakota populations today. Given that historical example, it would be prudent to remove that possibility from the discussion table. What the Israel example does offer, however, is the rationale for supporting the establishment of a safe haven in the homeland for a population of people that has been historically persecuted and subjected to policies of genocide and ethnic cleansing.

Minnesota's Wealth

Critics will point out the revenue that would be lost from such land return. However, an acknowledgment of that revenue only reveals that the injustices perpetrated against the Dakota people are ongoing; that is, Minnesotans are still getting wealthy at Dakota expense. When we acknowledge that Minnesotans established the state at Dakota expense, it means that Dakota people paid the price of genocide and ethnic cleansing so that Minnesotans could lay claim to all Dakota resources. It means that Minnesotans have drawn all the wealth out of Minnesota at Dakota expense. Theoretically, based on the wealth extracted from the state of Minnesota, Dakota people should be the wealthiest people in the state. Obviously, that is not the case.

Soybean field, Minnesota's rich agricultural lands. *Courtesy of Minnesota Historical Society.*

Aerial sprayer for agricultural fields. *Minneapolis Star Tribune. Courtesy of the Minnesota Historical Society.*

Log jam at Taylor's Falls, 1886. *Photo by Sanford C. Sargent. Courtesy of Minnesota Historical Society.*

Nine million feet of lumber piled 100 feet high, Boyle's Log Landing, 1894–95.
Courtesy of the Minnesota Historical Society.

For example, Minnesota's gross domestic product in 2005 was $234 billion.[20] In 2006, the gross domestic product was $244.5 billion.[21] According to Minnesota's Department of Employment and Economic Development, our approximately 27 million acres of farmland continue to be a huge source of reve nue. In 2003, for instance, Minnesota received $9.2 billion from agricultural sales. In 2005 Minnesota was the largest producer of sugar beets, sweet corn, green peas, and farm-raised turkeys. It was the second largest producer of spring wheat, canola, and cultivated wild rice and one of the top five producers of corn, soybeans, oats, dry edible beans, cheese, honey, and flaxseed. In addition, it was one of the top five producers of mink pelts, and hogs.[22]

Historically, timber has also been a major Minnesota resource. Exploitation of timber began commercially in Minnesota in 1839, building momentum as water-powered sawmills were replaced with steam-powered sawmills and band saws replaced circular

Akeley's Planing Mill, 1892. *Courtesy of the Minnesota Historical Society.*

saws. The annual harvest of timber was worth $2.5 million by the 1850s.[23] By the time of the peak of white pine logging in 1900, Minnesotans had an efficient system for resource extraction. Minnesotans harvested 2.3 billion board feet of lumber that year from our forests. They sustained that high level of exploitation for another ten years before yields began to decline and business

Mining industry, 1920 Hull Rust Mine. *Courtesy of the Minnesota Historical Society.*

Coal docks and equipment, Duluth 1915. *Photo by Charles P. Gibson. Courtesy of the Minnesota Historical Society.*

interests had stripped our white pine forests. By the 1930s the end of big-pine logging had come. While White entrepreneurs eradicated many of the white pines, remaining forests or refor- ested areas have kept a lumbering presence in the state.[24] In addition, wood products manufacturing and paper manufactur- ing are additional components of Minnesota's forestry industry.

Loading ore cars, 1935 Hull Rust Mine. *Courtesy of the Minnesota Historical Society.*

Minnesota resource exploitation, Hull Rust Mine, 1990. *Photo by David J. Nordgren. Courtesy of NMN, Inc.*

Mesaba pride in open pit mine and washing plant, 1960s Postcard. *Courtesy of NMN, Inc.*

Open pit mining, Biwabik 1885. *Courtesy of the Minnesota Historical Society.*

Remaining forests are still under threat by lumber interests. Winona LaDuke, for example, has articulated Anishinabe ongoing struggles with Potlatch, the largest clear-cutting lumber operation in the northwest region of the state that still threatens Minnesota's northern forests.[25]

Settler society has also extracted enormous amounts of mineral wealth from Dakota homeland. Today, Minnesota is the largest producer of the ferrous minerals natural iron ore and taconite in the United States.[26] In the 2006 production year, for example, Minnesota produced 39,297,977 taxable tons of taconite, meaning the production tax alone was $93,096,939 (at a rate of $2.2 per taxable ton).[27] Other industrial minerals such as aggregate (sand, gravel, and crushed stone), peat, kaolin clay, dimension stone, and silica sand, are also mined throughout the state. Aggregate is mined in nearly every county in the state, because aggregate materials are needed for widely used products such as concrete. Minnesotans mine other minerals more regionally. For example, Minnesotans mine kaolin clay in the Minnesota

River Valley to make cement, bricks, and tiles, and silica sand is mined in the southeastern portion of the state. Other minerals such as dimension stone (granite, gabbro, quartzite, and carbonate rock types) are used for home construction, buildings, and monuments.[28] According to the 2005 gross domestic product for Minnesota, the mining industry earned $896 million.

This is not to suggest that if Whites had not invaded and had instead left Dakota people to our homeland that, given sufficient time, we would have exploited the natural resources and built manufacturing companies to produce the kind of monetary wealth drawn out of the state today. In fact, I would suggest just the opposite. Left to ourselves, I think we would have continued to try to live according to the values of balance and reciprocity so that we could fulfill the cultural and spiritual ideal of *mitakuye owas'in*, all my relations. I think we would have attempted to ensure that our way of life remained sustainable. Frankly, I think Minnesota would be a much more healthy and beautiful place if Whites had not violently interfered in our relationship with the land and its beings. But, that is according to a Dakota value system. If, on the other hand, you value monetary wealth, greed, profit, domination over the land, and an unbridled hunger for new technology, you will think differently about what has transpired over the last 150 years. Is one value system inherently better than the other?

A Need for Change

In another age and context, Dakota People could have afforded to respect the differences in values and worldviews of other Peoples around the globe without making value judgments about those other ways of being or attempting to change them. In today's world, however, we cannot afford to take such a benign and tolerant approach. We all have to challenge the Western European ways of being that are leading everyone on a path to global catastrophe. Many of the values dominating the leading industrialized nations of the world are destructive to the planet and no one will be able to sustain them indefinitely. We simply will not survive if we continue on this harmful trajectory.

Even when we know the harmful effects of coal-fired power plants, for example, the U.S. continues to invest in creating new plants because the country's elite will not relinquish their opportunity to make millions, even billions of dollars. Rather than configuring the cost to the environment in discussions of affordable energy, corporations continue to sing the praises of "cheap" energy. You can only make such an assessment if you have already determined the expendability of the land, the animals, the plants, and the people who have to live in the contaminated regions downwind, downgrade, and downstream from coal-fired power plants, or if you ignore the escalating warming of the globe. Jeff Goodell, author of *Big Coal: The Dirty Secret Behind America's Energy Future*, details the harm created by these power plants, even after they have been "cleaned" up as a consequence of the 1970 Clean Air Act:

Nationwide, powerplants account for two-thirds of all sulfur dioxide, 22 percent of all nitrogen oxides, nearly 40 percent of carbon dioxide, and a third of all mercury emissions. Coal plants also release some sixty varieties of what the EPA terms "hazardous air pollutants," including known toxins such as lead (176,000 pounds), chromium (161,000 pounds), arsenic (100,000 pounds), and mercury (96,000 pounds). And that's just what goes in the air. Each year, coal plants produce about 130 million tons of solid waste—about three times as much as all the municipal garbage in the nation. This combustion waste—fly ash, bottom ash, scrubber sludge—is laced with heavy metals and other potentially toxic compounds and is routinely pumped into abandoned mines or impoundment ponds, where, if it is not handled correctly, it can leach into aquifers and water supplies."[29]

Similar reports could be made regarding various other industries including nuclear power, manufacturing, resource extraction industries (such as uranium mining), and particularly relevant to Minnesota, agribusiness. It is time we engage in an honest assessment regarding the failure of Western European values and ways of being that takes into account the environmental costs of American businesses. If we are to survive as human beings, we need to re-think our lifestyles and our relationship to the land.

As other scholars have pointed out, colonizing society viewed Indigenous Peoples as unworthy of the land precisely because we did not subdue the land, or establish dominion over the land.[30] The notion of subduing the land is fundamental to Judeo-Christian ways of conceiving the relationship between human beings and all of creation. Going back to the Book of Genesis, the *Bible* conveys this message repeatedly in various book verses. For example, Genesis 1:26 states, "Then God said, 'Let us make man in our image, in our likeness, and let them rule over the fish of the sea and the birds of the air, over the livestock, over all the earth, and over all the creatures that move along the ground.'" Genesis 1:28 states, "God blessed them and said to them, 'Be fruitful and increase in number; fill the earth and subdue it. Rule over the fish of the sea and the birds of the air and over every living creature that moves on the ground.'" The *Bible* repeats these teachings in the Books of Psalms, Jeremiah, and Daniel. Thus, the fact that most Indigenous Peoples did not practice this hierarchical and oppressive relationship with the rest of creation became a justification for taking Indigenous lands, using any means necessary. This notion formed the basis of Manifest Destiny ideology that sanctioned the invasion, theft, and ruthless exploitation of the Western hemisphere. This Judeo-Christian worldview, combined with capitalism's tenet of unrelenting resource exploitation, is largely responsible for the current global environmental crisis. It is most definitely responsible for the environmental desecration to Dakota homeland. This is exactly what needs to change.

One way to disrupt that worldview is to restore lands to Indigenous Peoples. This would permit Indigenous Peoples to reestablish the ways of being that allowed us to live sustainably for thousands of years while also modeling a different relationship with one another and the natural world based on principles of balance and respect. For Dakota people, Minnesota's ethnic cleansing policies severely compromised our relationship with our homeland. However, we first altered our relationship with the land with our participation in the fur trade, an exploitative economic endeavor based on treating animals as economic resources rather than as spiritual beings with whom we needed to maintain respectful relations. Obviously, colonizers did not initiate the fur trade because it was beneficial to Indigenous Peoples, but rather because it was a means for European and later Euro-American fur traders to accumulate wealth, at the expense of the animals, the land, and us. As has already been discussed, we can trace the wealth of some of Minnesota's founding fathers such as Sibley back to their exploitation of the fur trade. For Dakota people, gaining arms was of utmost importance to assist us in protecting our lands, and for the most part, our people were ignorant upon first contact about the cycles of dependency that would ensue. Ever since the fur trade, however, we have been caught in a global market that has challenged and compromised our ability to live according to what we generally consider as Dakota values.

Certainly, in a contemporary context, almost entirely disconnected from our original land base, colonizing society has prevented Dakota people from practicing the way of life originally given to us by the Creator. Colonizing society has prevented us from living according to our ideals. Furthermore, the struggle for basic survival has largely hindered our capacity to carry forward the environmental ethic central to our worldview. We have not adequately protected the land as we should have because we are frequently caught up in the oppressive forces that operate in our daily lives. And, pressures to survive economically have affected our decision-making about what is environmentally responsible within our own communities.

Thus, when we lay the issue of land return on the table, White Minnesotans question what Dakota people would do with reclaimed land. For example, in a presentation I gave on the *Take Down the Fort* campaign to a college class in St. Paul, one student raised his hand and asked what Dakota people would do with the Fort Snelling land base if it was restored to Dakota care. He eventually asked, "Would you want to put a casino there?" Given the reality that casinos provide the one intersection of ongoing interaction between Indigenous people and the dominant society in Minnesota, this question would probably be on the minds of most Minnesotans.

Recovery of Dakota Lifeways

It is at this point that this option differs markedly from the project of the "loyal Mdewakanton" lawsuit. While the lawsuit is committed to a small bit of land recovery, it is largely pursued, it appears, to gain wealth from casinos. The Constitution of the Minnesota Mdewakanton Dakota nation states that they are committed to the sustaining of Dakota culture and the encouraging of traditions, but because the lawsuit was their impetus for organizing, their claims are based on their self-declared superior right to the land, which works to exclude Dakota people who are not part of the "Loyal Mdewakanton." That agenda violates fundamental Dakota beliefs about inclusivity and recognition of all our relatives.

On the other hand, land recovery in the context that I am proposing is based on a commitment of the People to restore Dakota ways of being, including the organizing structures that existed in our society prior to colonization. Casinos, then, would not provide a desirable end goal, nor would material wealth.

Instead, what I would advocate is that land reparations would make available to Dakota people a place to come home. It would not be land set aside for those desiring to disavow Dakota tribal ties or to chase the American dream. Rather, it would be land for those Dakota people willing to invest themselves in the hard work of recovering Dakota ways of being, including a reclamation of our traditional systems of governance, our kinship system, our language, our spirituality, our subsistence practices, and an egalitarian, cooperative form of living communally. This is a project not designed for the fainthearted, shortsighted, or weakminded. It is a project that is designed for those Dakota people dissatisfied with the status quo, who hunger for a meaningful existence living, speaking, and dreaming as Dakota people.

This is not to suggest that we would reject everything from the modern world in favor of everything from our former, precolonized lives. Even if we wanted to, it would be extraordinarily difficult for us to live as we once did and to survive on the food sources that were the staples of our lives. Too much has changed in the landscape. The water, air, land, animals, and plants are all under siege from toxicity. Furthermore, settler society drove many of the animals that once inhabited our homeland to near extinction, just as we were. For example, elk and bison that we once depended upon as major food sources no longer run freely outside of cultivated herds in *Minisota*. The Anishinabe currently lay claim to many of our old ricing grounds, limiting our access to wild rice. Thus, it would be impossible for us to return immediately to a subsistence lifestyle. That way of interacting with the animals and land, however, would be a desirable end goal.

Because of the harm to the environment, and the ongoing threats that stem from our existence as part of a global community, it is imperative that as a collective community we remain aware of and skillful in new technologies. This pro-Dakota position is not in opposition to all technology, but it is a position that requires a critical interrogation of all technological "advancements." It would require a critical interrogation of technology that interferes with Dakota ways of being that have disconnected us from ourselves. This vision, at least initially, would maintain use of electricity, computers, and modern forms of housing, but we would have to design and utilize them in such a way as to be consistent with Dakota traditional values regarding sustainability.

Therefore, White Minnesotans need not fear that Dakota people would develop every part of Minnesota with casinos if settler society restored parts of our homeland to us, or that Dakota people would desecrate the environment. Such an argument is merely a projection of the dominant society's exploitative culture onto Dakota culture. It is not a reflection of Dakota culture. However, as we have learned, colonizer society has historically forced Dakota people to adopt methods and means of survival in the context of invasion, genocide, and dispossession of lands that are not always supportive of the Dakota environmental ethic. That is precisely why it is essential that settler society support Dakota people in our revitalization of our ancient ways of being. It is essential that settler society allow us to live according to our worldview on the lands that are our inheritance. White Minnesotans must help facilitate that recovery. That can best be achieved by restoring, at least, a significant portion of our homeland to us and helping us to restore the integrity of the land wherever it has been threatened. Dakota values and worldview do not allow for wide-scale development, but they do allow for interaction with and use of the land. This is not a threat to Minnesota's environment; this would help save it.

The Menominee forest reserves in Wisconsin offer one promising example of sustainable resource management. The Menominees have developed a sustained-yield forestry management system that has lasted more than 140 years along with wood-processing operations.[31] While visitors to their forests admire their pristine beauty, they describe how their forests are some of the most intensely managed ones in the lakes region, yet they remain an important resource. "During the last 140 years we have harvested more than two and one-half billion board feet of lumber from our land. That is the equivalent of cutting all the standing timber on the reservation almost twice over. Yet, the sawtimber volume now standing is greater than that which was here in 1854 when the Wolf River Treaty defined the Reservation."[32]

The White Earth Land Recovery Project (WELRP), founded by Winona LaDuke, provides another positive example regarding forest resource management. Certified by the Forest Stewardship Councils standards for a well-managed forest in 2003, their Sugarbush property demonstrates their commitment to conservation values as well as a continuation of Anishinaabeg cultural and spiritual practices. The WELRP is consequently able to harvest maple sugar sap, process it into maple syrup, and then market it directly through their business Native Harvest.[33]

Ideally, Minnesotans would return to Dakota people similar sugar-bushing stands in Minnesota sitting on lands currently identified as federal, state, or county lands, as part of a major reparations project. This would allow Dakota people to revitalize sugarbushing as a collective activity, restoring one of our traditional subsistence activities and reconnecting us with our homeland. It would also allow us to practice the environmental ethic that sustained us for millennia prior to invasion, ethnic cleansing, and colonization.

Future Land Return

While many public lands could be immediately restored to Dakota control, there are additional future possibilities to continue land restoration over the long-term. One possibility for ongoing land return is, ironically, in the category of tax-forfeited lands. This category represents the epitome of colonial practices. The U.S. federal government stole land from Indigenous Peoples, including Dakota land in Minnesota. Then, "As a part of Northwest Territories, Minnesota's land was granted by the federal government to private owners or the state as the state was settled."[34] The federal government then provided further land grants to the state to use for state purposes or to sell to private owners. Thus, when landowners today cannot pay required taxes, the lands are forfeited, most of them returning to the state for sale once again. The taxes collected on privately held land demonstrate the wealth still gained by local, state, and federal authorities for land wrested away from Dakota people. While the state currently holds about 2.8 million acres of tax-forfeited lands, this figure would continue to grow as the state continues to claim lands for reasons of tax forfeiture.

For example, in the period from 1926 to 1950, the state claimed somewhere between six and eight million acres of land through tax forfeiture.[35] The state resold most of that land, presumably keeping the revenue generated from those land sales, while consistently holding on to about one-third to one-half of those lands. Thus, in addition to the 2.8 million that Minnesotans could immediately return, Minnesotans could make a collective decision to return future tax-forfeited lands to Dakota people. Given the colonial nature of this enterprise of taxation on stolen Indigenous lands, this is a system that we will ultimately have to fundamentally challenge, but until that system is overturned, it is only reasonable to expect that it could be used as an instrument for righting a tremendous wrong.

In addition, private landowners can individually commit themselves to Indigenous land return. For example, a group informally known now as Whites for Native Land Return is having discussions now about how to institute a system for private land return to Dakota people in Minnesota. Some of these individuals are land holders without heirs and they recognize that they can personally contribute to addressing injustices by transferring their property to Dakota people upon their deaths, just as they might will their land, or revenue from land sales, to a specific organization or cause. Some also recognize that as individuals or families they would not be harmed by relinquishing some of their land holdings to Dakota control; that is, they have enough land for their family to live comfortably and they are consciously rejecting the notion that more is always better. This suggests that at least some people are reconsidering the *Monopoly* game mentality that requires mass accumulation of property and a need to build an empire of wealth, especially at other people's expense. They, in essence, can personally afford to commit themselves to justice. This group models decolonizing behavior by personally facilitating the reversal of Indigenous land dispossession and challenging the existing system of land tenure. This group will be initiating broader discussions about this process of Dakota land restoration in the coming years.

We can see examples of this personal commitment to justice for Indigenous Peoples in other colonial contexts, as well. For example, in 2007 the Victoria *Times Colonist* printed an article detailing the plans of local philanthropists. Bruce and Marion Cumming are transferring land title from their house situated on a one-acre, beautifully gardened plot of land in the upscale neighborhood of Oak Bay in Victoria, British Columbia, to Indigenous Peoples.* They are hoping that Indigenous artists and scholars might use the house as a retreat, especially the Coast Salish, as it is their traditional land upon which the house is built. The Cummings worked with Taiaiake Alfred (Mohawk), director of the Indigenous Governance Program at the University of Victoria, to create the Sacred Land Society that will set up directors to oversee the project and make sure that plans for the property are consistent with Indigenous values.[36] They offer a promising model for Indigenous land return, demonstrating that citizens can take restorative justice action even if governments are currently unwilling.

Additional Reparations

More than land reparations are needed to help right the historical wrongs perpetrated against Dakota people. Even if lands

---

*Bruce Cumming, unfortunately, passed away early in 2008, but his legacy to Indigenous Peoples will live on.

were available, few Dakota people would be able to pick up and move back to the homeland. We need to address many other factors in order to facilitate a Dakota migration home.

First, many Dakota people would need relocation expenses paid, as well as some kind of opportunity for paying off their existing debts. Second, upon arrival in the homeland, returning Dakota people would need an infrastructure in place, or they would need an opportunity to help create an infrastructure so their families would have basic needs met upon arrival including homes and water and power sources. Third, many of our people might need professional training in resource management so that we could work collaboratively with environmentally conscious outside agencies and organizations. While in previous centuries this would not have been a concern, in the contemporary world we must all closely monitor the environment so that we can address harms already perpetrated on the land and the animals, as well as determine changes occurring because of global warming. Like us, the land, animals, and plants have also faced horrendous colonization. They have a right to freedom from oppression as well. As the Original People, we have an obligation to assist in their liberation and care. Most of us do not currently have this kind of professional experience.

All Dakota people should be able to return to our homeland unencumbered by financial concerns that currently immobilize our populations. Given the way settler society has used capitalism as a weapon of oppression against Indigenous Peoples (beginning with the fur trade and continuing with the businesses that continue to exploit Indigenous communities, allowing their owners to grow wealthy while Indigenous people grow poor), this is not unreasonable.

The international movement for Third World debt cancellation offers a similar framework for discussion. World-renowned economist Jeffrey Sachs argues that the debts of heavily indebted poor countries (HIPCs) should not only be cancelled outright, but poor countries should never have been expected to repay them: "In fact, rich countries should have given the poorest countries grants rather than loans, so that the poor countries never would have been indebted in the first place."[37] He points out that this is the strategy the United States government employed in the formulation of the Marshall Plan after World War II. With a desire to not "encumber Europe's fragile democracies" at the conclusion of the war, U.S. strategists decided to administer grants rather than loans to rebuild Europe.[38]

The United States government and Minnesotans could employ a similar strategy to help ensure that rebuilt Dakota communities would begin with the strongest foundations, unencumbered financially. In the case of the Dakota, however, it would not be our debt to the government that would be repaid, rather it would be the government paying off debts accrued with banks, mortgage companies, and various businesses. This would help liberate our impoverished people from a system that has exploited us for centuries.

The U.S. government would also need to assist in relocation expenses. Given the violent way Minnesotans forcibly removed Dakota people from our homeland, reparative justice would demand that the U.S. government also provide the means for the safe return of our people to Minnesota. Such expenses might include assistance in wrapping up affairs in the old homes and assistance with packing, hauling, and transporting each family's belongings. Able-bodied Dakota people could assist in this process, but the U.S. government should provide the funds required to carry out the relocation.

Before families and communities begin arriving in Dakota homeland, it will be important to develop an infrastructure built according to Dakota environmental values. That is, from the very beginning, we should conceive of this migration home as a way of living Dakota principles and recovering Dakota life ways. While not dispensing with everything from the modern world, the necessary infrastructure should incorporate values of anti-materialism, a strong environmental ethic, and sustainability, all of which we could express in a communal living context.

This means that we should take care from the beginning to use green technologies and materials to build housing and to heat, cool, and produce necessary energy. Wind, solar, and geothermal technologies would all allow Dakota people to create self-sustaining communities where each person would take an active part in maintaining an ecological balance. Another aspect of the infrastructure would require accessing a sufficient clean water source for each community, such as digging wells and establishing pipelines. The communities could use compost toilets as a way to treat water as the valuable resource it is while also supporting larger composting efforts to help sustain agriculture and other plant growth. The building of these community infrastructures could be part of the larger Dakota reparations project.

Such an infrastructure would allow Dakota people to return, in families or communities, and immediately work to re-establish our ancient relationship to the Minnesota land base. Ideally, each community would have access to agricultural lands to implement ancient farming practices, and to wild-ricing grounds, sugar-bushing camps, hunting territories, and berry stands. The idea is that with access to traditional resources and the re-institution of a communal living ethic in which Dakota people would pool resources for the well-being of the whole, we would create self-sustaining communities.

This kind of sustainability would have other benefits as well. In the end, if we re-created the active lifestyles of our ancestors in terms of agriculture, hunting, and harvesting, and consequently became more active with healthier diets, many of the existing health problems in our communities might diminish with subsequent generations. In the meantime, our populations would need quality medical support and continued medical attention to address contemporary needs.

The Kanatsiohareke Model

We would establish these communities for a purpose similar to that of the traditional Mohawk community of Kanatsiohareke. A group of Mohawk families established this community in 1993 when, with donor help, they purchased through auction 322 acres of riverfront property. The establishment of this community al lowed some of those born in exile to return to their ancestral homeland in the Mohawk Valley near what is now Fonda, New York. As founder Tom Sakokwenionkwas Porter has described, "Kanatsiohareke is more than the realization of the prophecies of our elders; it also demonstrates the hope and determination for the rebirth of the traditional lifestyle of the Mohawks. It had long been our belief that we would need to do something dras-tic in order to survive. Thus, ours is a spiritual movement by Mohawk people who believe that the key to our survival rests in securing new lands and creating an environment conducive to practicing our traditional beliefs and culture and passing them on to our children and grandchildren."[39] Attempting to get away from the toxicity of the environment at Akwesasne (largely from PCB and mercury contamination caused by companies such as GM and Reynold's Aluminum), as well as the corruption from casinos, bingo halls, and cigarette smuggling, Porter and others sought healthful living through the recovery of Mohawk ways of being. They also sought peaceful co-existence with their non-Mohawk neighbors.

Today their community flourishes with over five acres of their traditional corn, 38 acres of hay, extensive gardens, fruit bushes, various trees, including maples for syrup-making, and sweet grass. They run a bed and breakfast, offer lectures, work-shops, and classes, as well as serve as a conference site and gath-ering place for various events including Mohawk immersion classes, spiritual gatherings, and art festivals (for both Mohawk and non-Mohawk populations).[40] They are attempting to undo the damage wrought to Indigenous communities under colonial rule and restore health and well-being to the Mohawk nation.

Rebuilding Our Communal Societies

The U.S. government worked systematically to break up our communal societies and this has been one of the most damaging aspects of colonialism. The divide and conquer tactics have created devastating factionalism, but there are other negative consequences of this eradication of community. First, it created a sense of selfishness and materialism and this was one of the intents behind the dismantling of Indigenous communities. One of the famous quotes by Senator Henry Dawes, the creator of the Allotment Act, illustrates this intent when discussing what he considered the defects of Indigenous communal societies: "There is no selfishness, which is at the bottom of civilization. Till this people will consent to give up their lands, and divide them among their citizens so that each can own the land he cultivates, they will not make much more progress."[41] Today, we must attempt to re-create the communal societies purposefully attacked and undermined by the U.S. federal government and its citizens. Recognizing the utter failure and immorality of American notions of "progress," we must embrace the communal values that underpinned our Dakota societies for millennia. It is there we will find strength and cohesiveness.

It is my hope that Dakota people will engage in rigorous and lengthy discussions regarding the reclamation of our homeland and that we will give significant time to the discussion of how we are to organize ourselves. We know that the current constitutional style governments based on the U.S. colonialist model has not served our people well. Our tribal council leadership is frequently fraught with corruption and few Dakota people are satisfied with the political status quo. Given that reality, it would make sense for us to reconsider the governmental structure that sustained us successfully prior to invasion and colonization. That would mean reinstituting the *Oceti Sakowin* as our governing structure and aligning ourselves according to specific villages that would make up the various bands composing the Seven Council Fires. Thus, a village might be predominantly Bdewakantunwan, but it might include individuals who have married in from other bands. Thus, we would work to maintain the distinct identities that made us Wahpetunwan, Sisitunwan, Bdewakantunwan, Wahpekute, or Ihanktunwan, but with an acceptance of, appreciation for, and interaction with the other fires.

Furthermore, such traditionally arranged communities would have a much more viable chance of completely reviving our languages and spirituality. One of the most urgent crises facing our communities today is the loss of language. While all our communities are engaged in various language recovery efforts, the diaspora of our people has inhibited the success of individual community efforts and our language continues to die. With the death of three fluent speakers in Minnesota in fall 2007, we now estimate that there are only ten fluent speakers of Dakota remaining in the state of Minnesota. While we will continue to fight courageously to save our language, it would have the best chance for survival if we brought our people home and lived in communal villages in which it became the dominant language of communication. Just as Jews gathered in Israel and revived Hebrew, so too could Dakota people gather in our homeland and revive our language.

Similarly, we will revive our oral tradition, ceremonies, dances, and other traditional knowledge more fully if they become a part of our daily practice as a community. For example, while living communally we could recover the practices regarding rites of passage, healing, and celebrations of life that at one time were part of our daily lives. We lost many of these practices in our communities because of communal breakdown accompanying colonization. Restoring these traditions would constitute a revaluing of all segments of our population and an investment in our happiness.

Because our traditions stem from the land on which we were created, it is in our homeland that they will flourish. Each new community could potentially serve as a healing center that would focus on all aspects of Dakota well-being. Like the community of Kanatsiohareke, we could also offer educational workshops in the areas of Dakota language, culture, and history, green technologies, and agricultural practices, and we could use the land as a gathering place for a variety of wellness events and programs.

What would separate such hypothetical communities from the communities we now inhabit is the intent of the people. At the heart of this vision for Dakota land reclamation is the belief that our people will flourish if we return to our original directions about how we are to live and learn to protect our homeland again. Thus, the reclaimed land would be dedicated to those Dakota people who are prepared to give themselves fully to the values and ways of being that make us distinctly Dakota. It would be a rejection of the values and ways of the dominant society that are harmful to our people, our lands, and our ways of being. This commitment to being Dakota would constitute nothing less than the rebirthing of our nation.

This vision is markedly different from what exists in our communities today. The individualism characterizing the dominant society is evident on our reservations and urban communities. This makes it virtually impossible to engage any project with a broad vision because community members cannot agree on much of anything. Thus, we have elections in our reservation communities in which people gain positions of power, not necessarily because the community as a whole supports them, but because they have a larger minority support base. Thus, there is always a large disgruntled population in the community and a tremendous sense of apathy. Frequently leaders who do the least damage (that is, no one can recount any major disasters associated with them) are often the ones who last in tribal office. This serves to maintain the status quo and squash any more radical projects that might fail and cause political disfavor for existing council holders. Leaders are forever walking a tightrope in which they try not to offend the most number of people.

Meanwhile, we gather for community functions, but the values and perspectives of individual members vary wildly, so there is little cohesiveness. Being Dakota in this context takes on an extremely fuzzy, mutable quality.

Ideally, reclaimed communities would counter this current condition and attempt to live according to Dakota worldview. This commitment to living according to Dakota values would therefore serve as a unifying force. Because many of us will have to relearn what this means, it will not occur without discussion and some disputes. Discussion and dispute resolution will be skills we will need to develop, just as we did centuries ago.

Furthermore, this is not a project for everyone. I do not recommend forcing anyone to participate in such a rebirthing of the Dakota Oyate. Many Dakota people may be perfectly comfortable in their lives, particularly those from wealthier gaming communities, and would not want to give up whatever privileges they might enjoy in their lives today. Or, many Dakota people may love the lands their families have now inhabited for generations and might not want to return to Minnesota. Others, perhaps, might have only a tenuous claim to Dakota identity and do not see a need for justice or for a rebuilding of the nation. That presents no conflict with those who would choose to return. Nothing would be stripped from any Dakota person who chose not to join a new community or move back to the homeland. When Jews returned to Israel, it was not by force. Similarly, we would not use force to compel Dakota relocation. Each individual or family would have to make that choice voluntarily. Those desiring to stay wherever they currently reside also need not suffer any negative repercussions. In fact, material conditions might even theoretically improve in older communities, as more lands would be available for those who remained behind. In addition, we would not exclude any Dakota people from these reclaimed communities as long as they adhered to a commitment to practice Dakota ways of being.

The Cost of Reparations Is Not Prohibitive

While the cost of reparations to Dakota people may initially seem outrageous, a broader context for comparison suggests these reparations are not outrageous at all. If we return to the example of Israel, we know that the U.S. generously assists nations it considers worthy of support. As one scholar has pointed out, "Total U.S. aid to Israel is approximately one-third of the American foreign-aid budget, even though Israel comprises just .001 percent of the world's population and already has one of the world's highest per capita incomes."[42] Our populations are also small, but each Indigenous nation does not receive this kind of economic support from the U.S. government. When we do receive relatively small amounts of money, it is characterized as welfare rather than aid to a worthy nation. The cost of reparations, however, becomes even more logically sound when we consider the enormous wealth that continues to be drawn from Dakota resources, while at the same time Dakota people are denied access to, or anything resembling just compensation for, those resources.

For example, in 2007 a federal magistrate ruled that the Treaty of 1805, in which two Dakota men ceded two nine-mile square blocks of land to the U.S. government for the piddling price of $2,000, was invalid. Though the Senate ratified the treaty, President Thomas Jefferson never signed the document.[43] According to our understandings of American legal principles, colonialist though they are, that means the U.S. government should return the land to Dakota people. That would be prime real estate in the Twin Cities metro area that Dakota people are denied today. For example, even if we took the value for the land estimated by Pike in 1805 as $200,000 and subtracted the $2,000 eventually given to Dakota people for that land, with 5 percent interest compounded annually, in 2008 the remaining amount due would be $3,963,628,125. If the U.S. government was going to compensate us fairly according to its own rules of justice, that would be almost $4 billion today. Or, if we used today's land values in the metro area for lands that Dakota people continue to be denied, the amount owed to the Dakota would likely be billions more. And that would only modestly address the first tiny land cession fraudulently taken by treaty.

Furthermore, if we rethink what will benefit all Peoples in terms of the environment, there are other ways the government can demonstrate its commitment to supporting the people who provide environmental services to the world, such as protecting biodiversity and reducing greenhouse gas emissions. For example, author Jeff Goodell has highlighted another way of looking at economic relations and natural resources. In 2005 at a UN conference on climate change, leaders from Papua New Guinea and Costa Rica suggested that other governments pay them to preserve the rainforest, since the forests serve as gigantic natural air filters and thus provide a service to the world. This was a concept backed by Nobel Prize–winning economist Joseph Stiglitz. Many villagers and local businesspeople continue to cut down the rainforests because they are desperately trying to make a living. If we instead made efforts to compensate people for protecting a natural resource that benefits the world, they could actively work toward those positive aims rather than yielding to actions they know are harmful simply because they need to put food on the table.[44] Similarly, given the destruction Minnesotans have unleashed on the land and the natural resources, particularly the forests, perhaps it would also make sense to compensate Indigenous Peoples in the state for natural resource preservation. Certainly all of us would benefit in the end from such environmental protections.

As Indigenous Peoples, we need to offer the world another way of being. As Dakota people, we can only do that if we are allowed a land base. It is time for all Minnesotans to recognize that Dakota people paid the price of statehood and to ask the question: What does recognition of genocide demand? In my mind, it demands reparative justice. This chapter has outlined one way of conceptualizing a program of Dakota justice. As you can see, it does not ask that all non-Dakota people leave our homeland, but it does require a major re-ordering of the existing structure. It is a vision just short of breaking camp. I hope you will join the conversation and begin to imagine for yourselves what justice would look like in this land of *Minisota*.

Notes

1. See the official Web site for the Minnesota Mdewakanton Dakota Oyate at http://www.freewebs.com/oyate/Aboutus.htm.

2. Arthur P. Rose, *An Illustrated History of Yellow Medicine County Minnesota* (Marshall, MN: Northern History Publishing Company, 1914), 45.

3. Kevin Diaz, "A 'great rift' widens," *Star Tribune*, April 22, 2007.

4. See United States Court of Federal Claims, No. 03-2684L, Section 2 Breach of Contract, p. 31.

5. Taiaiake Alfred, *Wasase: Indigenous Pathways of Action and Freedom* (Orchard Park, NY: Broadview Press, 2005), 22–23.

6. Diaz, "A great 'rift' widens," A10.

7. Ibid., A11.

8. Ibid., A11.

9. Charles Wilkinson, *Fire on the Plateau: Conflict and Endurance in the American Southwest* (Washington: Island Press, 1999), 132–47.

10. Wilkinson, *Fire on the Plateau*, 147.

11. Smith, *Conquest: Sexual Violence and American Indian Genocide*, 53.

12. These statistics are from "Minnesota Public Lands, 1983," a report prepared by the Land Management Information Center, Minnesota State Planning Agency, in cooperation with the Land Bureau, Minnesota Department of Natural Resources, November 1983. Through correspondence with the GIS Data Coordination Specialist at the Land

Management Information Center, I learned that this 1983 report has not yet been updated. However, other figures provided by the Minnesota Department of Natural Resources in their document, "The DNR Administered State-Owned Lands," and documents provided by the Minnesota Department of Administration including "A Historical Context for State Owned Lands in Minnesota" and "State Agencies With Custodial Control of Real Property (February 2007), Excluding MN State Colleges and Universities and University of Minnesota" corroborate the state-owned land figures used in the 1983 report within about 50,000 acres. A report copyrighted by the National Wilderness Institute, "State by State Government Land Ownership," however, states that the combined acreage of federal and state lands held in Minnesota are 11,975,000 acres, almost three million more acres than the "Minnesota Public Lands, 1983" report. Additional research is needed in this area.

13. See the Government of Nunavut Web site at http://www.gov.nu.ca/english/about/road.shtml.

14. See http://www.gov.nu.ca/hr/site/doc/nlca.pdf.

15. Leon Bram, Norma Dickey, eds., *Funk & Wagnalls New Encyclopedia* (Funk & Wagnalls Inc, 1986), volume 14, 297–311.

16. See http://www.mideastweb.org/us_supportforstate.htm (accessed January 28, 2008).

17. See http://www.trumanlibrary.org/whistlestop/study_collections/israel/large/index.php (accessed January 29, 2008).

18. USAID Budget for Israel," see www.usaid.gov/policy/budget/cbj2006/ane/il.html (accessed January 28, 2008).

19. See www.wrmea.com/html/us_aid_to_israel.htm.

20. Gross Domestic Product (GDP) by State 2005, see http://www.bea.gov/bea/newsrel/GSPNewsRelease.htm (accessed January 23, 2008).

21. See Energy Information Administration's Web site at http://tonto.eia.doe.gov/state/state_energy_profiles.cfm?sid=MN.

22. See http://www.deed.state.mn.us/whymn/resources.htm (accessed January 23, 2008).

23. Growth of Minnesota's Business and Industry on the State of Minnesota Yellow Pages Directory. See http://www.yellowpages.state.mn.us/is/yellowpages.nsf/58ff101d11e1f3d786256b2900205e6a/16e840 4dd4ce546286256b1f0059b802?OpenDocument.

24. See the Minnesota Historical Society's Web site: http://www.mnhs.org/places/sites/fhc/logging.html (accessed January 23, 2008).

25. Winona LaDuke, *All Our Relations: Native Struggles for Land and Life* (Cambridge: South End Press, 1999), 128.

26. See subheading "Metallic minerals," at the Department of Natural Resources Web site: www.dnr.state.mn.us/lands_minerals/mining.html (accessed January 23, 2008).

27. From the *Minnesota Mining Tax Guide*, Minnesota Department of Revenue, September 2007.

28. See subheading "Industrial minerals," at the Department of Natural Resources Web site: www.dnr.state.mn.us/lands_minerals/mining.html (accessed January 23, 2008).

29. Jeff Goodell, *Big Coal: The Dirty Secret Behind America's Energy Future* (Boston: Houghton Mifflin Company, 2006), 122–23.

30. For example, see Smith, *Conquest*, "Rape of the Land," 55–78, in which she agrees with the argument made by other feminist theorists that "there is a connection between patriarchy's disregard for nature, women, and indigenous peoples."

31. *Menominee Tribal Enterprises, Maeqtekuahkihkiw Kew Kanahwihtahquaq, "The Forest Keepers,"* The Menominee Forest-Based Development System, 1997, 8.

32. Ibid., 13.

33. See the White Earth Land Recovery Project's Web site at http://nativeharvest.com/node/4 (accessed January 29, 2008).

34. "A Historical Context for State Owned Lands in Minnesota," a document provided by the Minnesota Department of Administration, received January 25, 2008 from the Land Management Information Center.

35. Ibid.

36. Kim Westad, "Philanthropists envision their property as a retreat for First Nations artists," *Times Colonist,* Friday, March 30, 2007.

37. Jeffrey Sachs, *The End of Poverty: Economic Possibilities for Our Time* (New York: Penguin, 2005), 280.

38. Ibid., 280–81.

39. Tom Sakokweniankwas Porter, *Kanatsiohareke: Traditional Mohawk Indians Return to Their Ancestral Homeland* (The Kanatsiohareke Community, New York: 2006), originally printed in 1998, 41.

40. Ibid., 117–30.

41. Angie Debo, *And Still the Waters Run: The Betrayal of the Five Civilized Tribes* (Princeton: Princeton University Press, 1940), 22.

42. Stephen Zunes, "The Strategic Functions of U.S. Aid to Israel," www.wrmea.com/html/us_aid_to_israel.htm.

43. Bill Clements, "Court Ruling Does Little To Settle Fort Snelling Debate," Dolan Media Newswires, January 4, 2007.

44. See Jeff Goodell, *Big Coal: The Dirty Secret Behind America's Energy Future*, (Boston: Houghton Mifflin Company, 2006), 245–46.

FIVE

Developing Peaceful Co-Existence

*To remain true to a struggle conceived within
Onkwehonwe [Original People] values, the end
goal of our Wasase—our warrior's dance—must be
formulated as a spiritual revolution, a culturally
rooted social movement that transforms the whole
of society and a political action that seeks to remake
the entire landscape of power and relationship to
reflect truly a liberated post-imperial vision.*

— TAIAIAKE ALFRED, *WASASE*[1]

In order to create a society dedicated to peaceful co-existence,
oppression in all its forms must end—particularly forms of oppression that have been institutionalized. Thus, we must begin by
implementing acts of reparative justice that will ensure a homeland for Dakota people as well as ensure an infrastructure that
will support Dakota ways of being. Then, we also must expose
and overturn all the institutions that allow for the systematic
exploitation of people and resources, the oppression of groups,
and the degradation of the environment. We must eradicate
the relationship between the colonizer and the colonized and
overturn the institution of colonialism. Finally, we must replace
those harmful ways with systems and ways of living that are respectful to all of creation.

Assessing Our Values

As a beginning, we need to examine the underlying value assumptions that guide our personal lives and assess whether we

are fulfilling those values at the broader, public level. When a group of Dakota people developed our presentation for the Minnesota Sesquicentennial Commission to address the history of genocide and ethnic cleansing, we began with a discussion of the values that were informing our presentation. They included:

- Genocide is a crime against humanity.
- Might is not right.
- White is not right.
- The only good society is a just society.

Few Minnesotans would outwardly disagree with those values. They represent values that most of us attempt to teach our children. Yet, when we examine Minnesota history and the treatment of Dakota People, we can see that Minnesotans have failed to live up to those values in regards to Dakota People.

Thus, we need to determine collectively what values and goals will allow us to move toward a peaceful and sustainable future. For example, most people would not embrace oppression as a core value they try to uphold. Most of us like to think of ourselves as "good" human beings and we do not self-identify as oppressors. Yet, oppression occurs every day, sometimes in our families, certainly in our local communities, and in the state more broadly. What this means is that there is a disconnect between the way we see ourselves and the way we operate as a collective society. We need to consider a dramatic rethinking of the way we exist in this world. Do the values we hold allow for the oppression of other people or the environment? Are they sustainable in the long term? That is, when we implement those values, will they contribute to global destruction, or can we practice them sustainably? Prior to colonization, most Indigenous societies in North America had developed a means for sustainable living. This is not to suggest that there were no examples of societies that rose and fell or that there were no periods of turmoil and imbalance, but most societies had mechanisms for restoring balance. Our ancestors placed value on the notion of balance as it represented the ideal way of being in this world. Given the fact that we are all part of a global community in which our actions affect the lives of others, we can no longer afford to allow some segments of the population to pursue an agenda that might harm the rest of us. This means we need to abandon fundamental institutions in North America—even the current system of government.

Andrea Smith articulates in her work the need to not only dispel familiar myths regarding the permanency of the American nation-state, but also that we must rework the existing social order. Smith points out the extent of injustice embedded within America's foundation: "The 'freedom' guaranteed to some individuals in society has always been premised upon the radical unfreedom of others. Very specifically, the U.S. could not exist without the genocide of Indigenous Peoples. Otherwise visitors to this continent would be living under Indigenous forms of governance rather than U.S. empire."[2] Thus, if all of America is based on the fundamental denial of freedoms (including the right to life) to Indigenous Peoples, then any attempt toward justice must consider the elimination of the U.S. government as a political entity. Smith further argues that because of the oppression embedded in the existing political structure, we also "need to think beyond the nation-state as the appropriate form of governance for the world."[3]

Similarly, capitalism, as it exists in America, needs to be overturned. We must challenge any system in which profit making is the primary objective. The capitalist system is designed so individuals and corporations can amass wealth, while ignoring the costs to other humans and the environment. If we consider how Indigenous Peoples in the U.S. have suffered because of our capitalist economic system, for example, it is clear that capitalism is not a system under which everyone can benefit, no matter how many jobs we hold or how hard we work. Instead, those who benefit the most are those who accrue wealth by exploiting the resources of everyone while at the same time denying responsibility for public interests. The largest beneficiaries of capitalism are willing to pass on devastating costs to society and to the future generations who will inherit our desecrated planet. Furthermore, because we currently base our capitalist system on the exploitation of people and finite resources, the current model of consumerism and materialism is, simply, impossible to sustain. Our oil-based civilization is quickly ending.

Some of the most progressive and promising models for sustainability involve localizing economies, including localizing food and energy production and consumption. While such a movement does not mean a total rejection of global community engagement, it does require a critical look at our relationships with our neighbors, the land, and the other beings that inhabit our environment. It compels a conscious awareness of our environmental footprint and a subsequent desire to keep that footprint as small as possible. When we look to meet our needs and solve our problems at the local level, we foster within ourselves a sense of love for and a desire to protect our local communities. This is how we might all work toward peaceful co-existence in Dakota homeland.

Eventually, we would need to overturn every other system and institution currently oppressive to Dakota people. The extent to which the systems continue to fail or harm our people is evident in our social circumstances. Our students continue to drop out of mainstream educational facilities at extraordinarily high rates across the board. Given the educational systems dedication to creating "good citizens" and conformity to American values, it is no wonder. Rather than fostering critical thinking and embedding values that reflect a concern for all life, the educational system continues to perpetuate Manifest Destiny ideology that justifies Indigenous killing and land theft as well as blind obedience to the existing social order.

Similarly, the social welfare system, like the criminal (in)justice system, continues to break up families. Rather than working to overturn a fundamentally unjust system, social workers continue to blame families for problems, as if individuals are acting in a vacuum. Meanwhile, Indigenous children and adults are judged and sentenced more harshly and serve disproportionately higher rates of incarceration for longer sentences. When substance abuse and family violence ravage our communities, the system tells us that we are to blame, rather than the society and institutions that continue to dehumanize and oppress Indigenous Peoples and denigrate everything Indigenous.

Furthermore, the existing health care system is highly problematic because it continues to focus on treatment for disease and poor health, rather than on preventative, holistic care that incorporates Indigenous practices. While we desperately require top-notch health care today because of all the threats to our bodies as a consequence of colonialism, our health will be restored more fully when we can begin to strengthen ourselves by recovering the healthy ways of living that sustained us prior to colonization. We must eventually abandon the oppressive institutions in favor of those that fully support Indigenous Peoples and Indigenous ways of being.

A Message to Dakota People

At the conclusion of the 2002 Dakota Commemorative March, Clifford Canku, a Sisseton elder and one of our spiritual leaders from the March, articulated what many of us felt regarding being on the verge of new possibilities. His words of empowerment were expressed in his comments, "We don't need to be complacent anymore. . . . I think it's time that we risk bravery and say 'this is what we feel, this is what we need to do,' and get it done, do it. . . . We're living in exciting times and we need to vision for our people."[4]

Our colonizers told us that we must accept the way things are because we cannot change them. They have told us that because they are invested in maintaining the colonial status quo and because they continue to benefit from the ongoing denial of justice to our people. More specifically, they are benefiting from Dakota lands and resources and they do not want us to imagine a future in which we have reclaimed our homeland. As revolutionary intellectual Frantz Fanon wrote, "The settler's work is to make even dreams of liberty impossible for the native."[5] Thus, it is settler society in the U.S. that has constrained our imaginations regarding what is possible, even within our own homeland.

Our task as Dakota people, then, is to expand our minds and carry our thinking to the farthest possible extension, and to imagine a world profoundly different from the one we currently inhabit. We need to imagine a decolonized world free from oppression. More importantly, we need to engage in discussions within our own communities and help unleash our collective intellectual imaginations. We need to envision decolonization first and then work toward achieving it.

Michael Yellow Bird and I stated in the introduction to the Decolonization Handbook, "As Indigenous Peoples we have an inherent right to be free in our own lands. We have an inherent right to self-determination. When others invaded our lands and stole them from underneath our bodies, when they destroyed our ways of life and injured our peoples, we were prevented from living the way we were intended to live."[6] Now, the struggle in our era is first to begin a collective remembering of those ways of being that were intended for us as Dakota people, and then to develop intelligent and calculated strategies to recover them so that we may eventually achieve our own liberation. How many of you can imagine a time when the Dakota Oyate will be free once again? Do you believe it is possible? Or does our freedom only come with our death in this world? Can you imagine our own liberation on earth? If you cannot, freedom will remain an elusive possibility. However, if you can imagine a liberated future, then we have somewhere to go and we have a lot of work to do.

Once we reject complacency as a reasonable course of action, we realize the abundant opportunities for revolutionary change around us. For the sake of clarity, I think it is important to state that I think our work toward revolutionary change should serve the purposes of decolonization. By decolonization, I mean "the intelligent, calculated, and active resistance to the forces of colonialism that perpetuate the subjugation and exploitation of our minds, bodies, and lands" and that "decolonization is engaged for the ultimate purpose of overturning the colonial structure and realizing Indigenous liberation."[7] I believe that we will best achieve decolonization by recovering the ways of being and living that sustained us as Dakota people for thousands of years. The struggle for decolonization requires us to identify clearly our objectives and to critically question whether they are constrained by the parameters of thought set by colonialism, or whether they traverse those parameters and reflect our desires as free, Indigenous Peoples of the land. We can be free, but only if we first imagine, and then seek our freedom.

A Message to Wasicu (White) People

Given the current educational system in the state of Minnesota, indeed, in the United States, most of you have never learned the truth regarding the founding of the United States. Nor have you learned how each state systematically dispossessed Indigenous Peoples of our homelands in order to claim Indigenous land bases. Even in Minnesota, where the U.S.–Dakota War of 1862 is included in the state's curriculum standards, we do not learn the broader context for, and the ideology underpinning, the war. That is, students today do not learn about concentration camps, genocide, ethnic cleansing, or bounties, which are all part of the policies of extermination and forced removal advocated by Alexander Ramsey and implemented by Minnesota's citizens. Students do not learn that most Dakota people still live in exile and that Dakota people today possess only .006 percent of our original land base. That lack of education, or even miseducation, means that adult citizens in the state cannot conceive of justice for Dakota people, because they do not even recognize the injustice.

I do not believe that (non-Dakota) Minnesotans are inherently evil or bad people. In fact, I believe Minnesotans are people who want to be on the right side of a moral issue. Yet, genocide is not moral and what was gained because of genocide is not moral. Minnesotans have the capacity to make radical change once they understand the history and the need to work for justice. All of you reading this can no longer claim ignorance.

It could be that this information will not move some of you—that the same kind of genocidal thinking that prevailed in nineteenth-century America is flourishing in your minds. If that is so, I do not believe you are in the majority. I would like to believe that something has changed in 150 years and that today's Minnesotans do not want to continue to deny justice to Minnesota's Original People. I hope I am right.

Decolonization requires the creation of a new social order, but this would ideally be a social order in which non-Dakota would also live as liberated peoples in a system that is just to everyone, including the land and all the beings on the land. Thus, *Wasicu* people need not fear the empowerment of Dakota people. When we are lifted up and our humanity is recognized, everyone will be lifted up. Those of us clinging to traditional Dakota values are not interested in turning the tables and claiming a position as oppressor, as colonizer, or of ruthlessly exploiting the environment for profit. Thus, what Fanon wrote about the Third World rising and the expectations of Europe might also be applied to the Indigenous struggle in North America: "What it expects from those who for centuries have kept it in slavery is that they will help it to rehabilitate mankind, and make man victorious everywhere, once and for all."[8] All of you today are in a position to help us rehabilitate humankind, but it has to start here. Right here, in Dakota homeland.

Minnesota River. *Photo by Waziyatawin.*

Final Thoughts

This project was motivated out of a desire for social change—a change that would allow for the return of Dakota people to our homeland and for the rebirth of the Dakota Oyate in our homeland. This is, at heart, a spiritual motivation because it calls on Dakota people to strengthen our spiritual relationships with all of creation so that we can return to healthy ways of being. It also is spiritual in that it calls on the people who have benefited from Dakota dispossession to help repair tremendous harms, so that we can all live together in a good way. This cannot proceed as long as Minnesotans deny this legacy of genocide and ethnic cleansing, or if Minnesotans continue to celebrate what was gained from our genocide and dispossession. If we eventually reach a place in which we have repaired the injustice and restored the integrity of the land and people, then all Minnesotans will really have something to celebrate. In the meantime, we have a lot of work to do.

Notes

1. Taiaiake Alfred, *Wasase: Indigenous Pathways of Action and Freedom* (Orchard Park, NY: Broadview Press, 2005), 27.

2. Smith, *Conquest*, 184.

3. Ibid., 184.

4. See Clifford Canku's comments in Waziyatawin Angela Wilson, "Voices of the Marchers" in *American Indian Quarterly* 28, no. 2 (Winter/Spring 2004): 333.

5. Frantz Fanon, *Wretched of the Earth* (New York: Grove Press, 1963), 93.

6. Waziyatawin Angela Wilson and Michael Yellow Bird, *For Indigenous Eyes Only: A Decolonization Handbook* (Santa Fe: School of American Research Press, 2005), 1.

7. Ibid., 5.

8. Fanon, *Wretched of the Earth*, 106.

Index

Waziyatawin is a Wahpetunwan Dakota from the Pezihutazizi Otunwe
(Yellow Medicine Village) in southwestern Minnesota. She received
her Ph.D. in American history from
Cornell University in 2000 and
spent seven years teaching in the
history department at Arizona State
University. After earning tenure and
an associate professorship at ASU,
she left the academy in 2007 to work
as an independent scholar. Waziyatawin is the author of *Remember*

This! Dakota Decolonization and the Eli Taylor Narratives (University of Nebraska Press, 2005) and co-editor of *Indigenizing
the Academy: Transforming Scholarship and Empowering Communities* (University of Nebraska Press, 2004) and *For Indigenous Eyes Only: A Decolonization Handbook* (School of America
Research Press, 2005).

Her most recent volume, *In the Footsteps of Our Ancestors* (St.
Paul: Living Justice Press, 2006), is an edited collection that tells
the stories, both in words and pictures, of the Dakota Death
Marches of 1862 and the commemorative walks that have been
held in recent years to honor the memory of those Dakota people
who endured the 1862 forced removals. That volume was the re-
cipient of the 2007 Independent Publisher's Silver Book Award
for Adult Multicultural Non-fiction.

Waziyatawin is founder and director of Oyate Nipi Kte, a nonprofit dedicated to the recovery of Dakota traditional knowledge,
sustainable ways of being, and Dakota liberation. Waziyatawin holds
the Indigenous Peoples Research Chair in the Indigenous Governance Program at the University of Victoria in British Columbia.
Most of the year she resides in the Minnesota River Valley.

About Living Justice Press

A 501(c)(3) tax-exempt, nonprofit publisher on restorative justice

Living Justice Press (LJP) publishes books about social justice and community healing. We focus specifically on restorative justice and peacemaking, and within this field, we concentrate our work in three areas.

First, we publish books that deepen the understanding and use of peacemaking Circles. Circles help people deal with conflicts and harms in ways that promote justice and "being in a good way" as a way of life. Indigenous in origin, Circles are proving to be transformative for people across cultures, age groups, genders, and nationalities. Youth in particular blossom in the spaces that Circles create.

Second, because restorative justice draws directly from Indigenous philosophies and practices, we publish on Indigenous ways of understanding justice. These ways generally have to do with learning "how to be good relatives"—not only with each other but also with the peoples of the natural world.

Third, we publish the voices of those "in struggle" for justice. Our books seek to apply what we have learned about healing harms between people to the larger and more systemic challenges of addressing harms between peoples. Through our publishing, we join in working toward justice between peoples through paths of education, exploring how to rectify harms, and transforming our ways of being together. According to restorative justice, this journey begins with hearing the stories—especially from those whose voices have not been heard—and finding out from those who suffered what it would take to "make things right."

This book falls in the third area. Responses to its ideas will certainly span the spectrum—not only from people in non-Dakota communities but from those in Dakota communities as well. The subject is controversial—inevitably so, given our shared history.

Our aim in publishing this book is to "hold a space" where a dialogue can begin between those who have suffered great harms and those who benefit from them, however unaware of the cost to others we may have been.

Given a past filled with violence and injustices and their ongoing legacies, restorative justice spurs us to ask: What happened? Who has been hurt? Who is still hurting? What stories do we need to hear that we have not heard? What might it take for us to be together in a good way now? That is, what practical, concrete steps can we take to come to terms with how we got to where we are and to put things right? And, what good might we all gain by embarking on this journey?

In this context, debating this position or that proposal is secondary to engaging in a process that is fundamentally about doing justice, so that we can coexist peacefully and with mutual respect. This positive process begins with hearing voices that are often not heard precisely because they are not easy to hear. If the blending of anger with truth makes the hearing rough, it generally helps to imagine what emotions we might feel were we in the same position—if our ancestors had suffered this treatment and our relatives continued to struggle as a result. How could anger not be an appropriate response to atrocities and injustices committed against families and communities?

Hearing such painful stories is never easy, though, and it is all the more difficult when our way of life is directly related to the sources of pain. Nonetheless, it is where the journey of addressing harms begins. Hearing the stories creates spaces for transformation on all sides, so that we can take steps toward being "in a good way" with each other.

Given the power of this dialogue and the need for it, with this book, we at Living Justice Press are initiating a series on the theme of what justice looks like from the point of view of various people, peoples, histories, and current realities.

As we all know, our past is filled with massive systemic harms that directly shape our present—who continues to possess the land, wealth, and power and who continues to struggle to get by. The state-sponsored crimes and terrorism perpetrated against the Dakota People were replicated against Native Peoples across the continent in order to steal Native lands coast to coast.

Similarly, the holocaust of slavery was about stealing what is most personal and precious to human beings: our labor. Douglas A. Blackmon's *Slavery by Another Name: The Re-Enslavement of Black Americans from the Civil War to World War II* is one of the latest books to document horrific crimes perpetrated against African Americans. Local, state, and federal governments colluded with White citizens, corporations, and other institutions to arrest and convict innocent Black men in order to obtain cheap convict labor for industry—at the cost of unimaginable human suffering to the men and their families. Today, the criminal justice system continues to arrest and imprison people of color disproportionately, and corporations continue to exploit cheap convict labor.

Given this systemic terrorism carried out against peoples of color over centuries with legacies that continue today, "What does justice look like?" stands as a compelling question. In restorative justice processes, this question is acknowledged as critical for resolving harms between individuals, yet it is often the sticking point for addressing harms between peoples. It is precisely this question that this book and the books to follow address.

Because the notion of actually doing justice has seemed so remote to so many for so long, our parameters for thinking about what could be done tend to narrow, bound by how things have been. Restorative justice is about bringing people together to think about justice in new and fundamentally different ways— ways that actually feel like justice to those who have suffered. If "just us" is not justice, but if "just us" has been the rule, the norm, how can we do justice in ways that respect everyone and that feel like justice to all those who share a history on this continent?

We therefore invite readers and other authors to engage the

painful stories of collective injustices and then to explore our potentials for doing justice today. Clearly, no one of us has all the answers for how to right immense harms, but we can open the dialogue. We can hear the stories that have been excluded or dismissed. And then we can use our creativity to imagine what can be done to "make things right." What are our options for doing justice now, and how can we move positively and concretely in these directions?

With Waziyatawin, we wish to express our gratitude to the Dakota and non-Dakota people who donated to Living Justice Press specifically to support the publication of this book. These include the Upper Sioux and Lower Sioux Dakota Communities, the Minnesota Humanities Center, the HRK Foundation, the Patrick and Aimee Butler Family Foundation, and the Archie D. and Bertha H. Walker Foundation. We also want to express our special gratitude to Wendy Holdman for donating the many hours she has spent typesetting this book. As Waziyatawin wrote in the opening pages, these individuals, communities, and organizations do not necessarily support all the views that she expresses, but they do support the need to give voice to the often-ignored perspectives of Indigenous Peoples.

We also want to thank those of you who provide ongoing support to Living Justice Press by buying our books, using them for groups and classes, making financial donations, as well as donating your time through volunteer work. We continue to exist through your generosity and vision. And we are most grateful to those of you who spend time reading the books we publish, pondering their ideas, and using them in your work for justice. You are our inspiration. Thank you!

Living Justice Press
2093 Juliet Avenue, St. Paul, MN 55105
Tel. (651) 695-1008 • Fax. (651) 695-8564
E-mail: info@livingjusticepress.org
Web site: www.livingjusticepress.org

Books from Living Justice Press

On the Circle Process and Its Uses

Peacemaking Circles: From Crime to Community by Kay Pranis, Barry Stuart, and Mark Wedge, ISBN 0-9721886-0-6, paperback, 271 pages, index.

Building a Home for the Heart: Using Metaphors in Value-Centered Circles by Pat Thalhuber, B.V.M., and Susan Thompson, foreword by Kay Pranis, illustrated by Loretta Draths, ISBN 978-0-9721886-3-0, paperback, 224 pages, index.

Peacemaking Circles and Urban Youth: Bringing Justice Home by Carolyn Boyes-Watson, ISBN 978-0-9721886-4-7, paperback, 296 pages, index.

On Indigenous Justice

Justice As Healing: Indigenous Ways, edited by Wanda D. McCaslin, ISBN 0-9721886-1-4, paperback, 459 pages, index.

On Addressing Harms between Peoples

In the Footsteps of Our Ancestors: The Dakota Commemorative Marches of the 21st Century, edited by Waziyatawin Angela Wilson, ISBN 0-9721886-2-2, oversize paperback, 316 pages, over 100 photographs, color photo insert, index.

What Does Justice Look Like? The Struggle for Liberation in Dakota Homeland by Waziyatawin, ISBN 0-9721886-5-7, paperback, 150 pages (approx.), index.

We offer a 20% discount on orders of 10 books or more. We are delighted to receive orders that come directly to us or through our Web site. Our books are also available through amazon.com, and they can be special ordered from most bookstores. Please check our Web site for announcements of new LJP books.

Order by phone, fax, mail, or online at:

2093 Juliet Avenue, St. Paul, MN 55105
Tel. (651) 695-1008 • Fax. (651) 695-8564
E-mail: info@livingjusticepress.org
Web site: www.livingjusticepress.org